God's Grace For Your Career

Unwrapped

Learning Guide

Katie Conley

ENDORSEMENTS

God's Grace
For Your Career
Unwrapped
Learning Guide

Katie Conley

Ladey
Adey
Publications

COPYRIGHT

DEDICATION

'And God is able to make all grace abound to you,
so that having all contentment in all things at all times,
you may abound in every good work'
(2 Corinthians 9:8 ESV).

This Learning Guide is dedicated to anyone who is serious about pursuing God and unwrapping the GRACE He has given them for their career so they can use their gifts, relationships, abilities, curiosities and experiences in service to other people and the world around them to His eternal glory.

May you feel God's inspiration as you explore God's GRACE for your career and may you partner with Him in your career each and every day.

CONTENTS

Contents

Introduction

Gifts
Relationships
Abilities
Curiosities
Experiences

GRACE

INTRODUCTION

'May the grace of the Lord Jesus be with God's holy people'
(Revelations 22:21 NLT).

God has given you all the GRACE you need for your career, even though you may not realise this. He has given you ....

- ❀   Gifts, both natural and spiritual.

- ❀   Relationships with God and other people.

- ❀   Abilities, including your talents, skills and strengths.

- ❀   Curiosities about the world, providing clues for your career choices.

- ❀   Experiences, understanding God uses everything, both good and bad.

My book God's GRACE for Your Career explores each of these areas through Bible stories and verses, prayers, interviews with Christians about their career perspectives and activities to help you discover your own career purpose.

This learning guide is designed as an accompaniment to the book, giving you space and time to write down your reflections and complete the activities in one convenient place. As you work through it you will build up a picture of everything God has given you and you will be able to make career decisions and choices based on all the information you gather about yourself.

How the learning guide is set out

Each module encourages you to read the corresponding chapter in the main book. Then you have space to record your thoughts and complete the activities and the reflection activities at the end of each section, using the questions and prompts to guide you.

God's GRACE for Your Career

'For you created my inmost being; you knit me together in my mother's womb.
(Psalm 139:13).

You will see from the Introduction the premise for the book is built on the parable of the Prodigal Son (Luke 15:11-32) which demonstrates God's grace at work in each of our lives. I share my own faith story and then explain how God has made each of us individually, with a unique package of gifts, talents, skills and aptitudes that make up 'you'.

The uniqueness God has given you is packaged with GRACE and this acronym provides the modules for this learning guide to help you unpack what He has given you. This is not always a neat package of uniqueness. There are overlaps and gaps and sometimes it looks a bit messy. However, it is being skillfully woven by God, who sees the end result long before you do.

Because it's messy and different for everyone and it takes time to make sense of your individual knitting you might find you spend more time completing some activities than others. You might spend considerable time pondering your natural gifts, or considering your dreams, or you might jump straight ahead to explore your values or see what's in your Vine of Curiosity.

Your career is individual to you. The way you do your work is also individual to you, even if you are stacking shelves, feeding cattle or running a corporation, God has filled you with GRACE for your career. He can provide meaning to what you do when you understand the GRACE He has given you.

Ken Costa writes, "The better we know ourselves, the more we can imagine what kind of work God might be calling us to"[1]. So, I invite you to get to know yourself better, to explore the GRACE God has given you for your career. I hope you will realise, as I have, that God has been at work in your career effecting His plan through all the highs and lows, and that His grace is more than enough.

Grace is God's undeserved love for us. It's His unconditional love. We cannot earn God's grace. It is His free gift, given to us through the death and resurrection of Jesus on the cross. We receive it when we return to God, when we repent, turn away from our sin, and put our faith in Jesus. Paul writes in Romans 10:9, 'If you declare with your mouth, "Jesus is Lord," and believe in your heart that God raised him from the dead, you will be saved'.

My prayer is for you to be blessed as God reveals your own package of GRACE, that you would gather strands of gold in the knitting that makes up your personal embroidery and along the way discover God's blueprint and purpose for your future career.

Prayer
Father God, thank You for the GRACE You have given me for my career. Guide me through Your Holy Spirit as I explore the Gifts, Relationships, Abilities, Curiosities and Experiences that make up the unique package of GRACE for my career.
In Jesus Name, Amen.

Write your own prayer here.

1

Gifts

Relationships
Abilities
Curiosities
Experiences

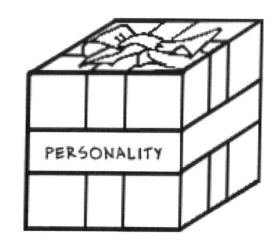

MODULE 1 - GIFTS

'Every good and perfect gift is from above, coming down from the Father
of the heavenly lights, who does not change like shifting shadows'
(James 1:17).

God is excited about the gifts He has given you for your career! They are carefully selected to fit your character, personality and your inner self, and bring joy to your heart. Father God has wrapped these gifts up for you and longs to watch you unwrap them. God has chosen gifts specifically for you, befitting the role He has in mind for you. Sometimes we find it hard to find these gifts, let alone accept them, but I encourage you to take the time to try to find out what they are.

In this module you'll start by exploring the gifts God gave you as a child, your Natural Gifts. These are the actions and behaviours you find easy and come naturally to you. They are the building blocks of your abilities. You will consider your Personality, and the components God has used in making you who you are. Then you will dream Dreams! What dreams do you have for your career? Finally, you'll review your Spiritual Gifts and consider how God might want you to use them in your career.

It's time to go on a journey to unwrap the gifts God has given you. Gifts come in many shapes and sizes, and God will keep giving you gifts throughout your career.

Prayer
Father God thank You for all the gifts You have given me – help me to find them
and unwrap them so that I can use them for Your glory.
In Jesus name, Amen.

Write your own prayer here.

YOUR NATURAL GIFTS

'Each of you should use whatever gift you have received to serve others,
as faithful stewards of God's grace in its various forms'
(1 Peter 4:10).

Read the section on YOUR NATURAL GIFTS in the book.

Make a note of your reflections and thoughts here.

Discover your own natural gifts.

God has left clues for you to find about the natural gifts He has given you. They are evident in the things you used to love to do as a child, the times when you felt fully absorbed in some activity doing whatever felt totally natural to you.

You might not be doing these things anymore, but your natural gifts will give you clues about how God has gifted you naturally.

Exploring the natural gifts God has given you starts by reviewing the patterns of things you used to do easily as a child. Then as you mature these natural gifts grow into abilities such as talents, skills and strengths, which you will explore in Module 3.

ACTIVITY I:
WHAT ARE YOUR NATURAL GIFTS?

Purpose

To identify Your Natural Gifts.

Prayer

Father God thank you for the natural gifts I was born with,
the things You gave me at birth, the things I naturally find easy to do.
As I make a note of them now remind me of anything I may have forgotten.
In Jesus Name, Amen

Instructions

1. Use the questions below to prompt your memory and write down anything that comes to mind.

❋   What did you really enjoy doing as a child? Did you like playing with friends, toys or on your own?

❋   What things were you naturally drawn to? This could be things like people, pets, the outdoors, music.

❋   Did you like music, sport, art, design, sewing, gardening, reading, writing, shopping, talking, watching, listening, building things, exploring technology? What other things did you like?

✸ What games did you play as a child? Hide and seek, tag, make believe, dressing up, on your own or with other people?

✸ What were your favourite toys? If you played with Lego©, did you prefer to make people or buildings? If you played with dolls or stuffed toys what did you do with them? Did you care for them or organise them?

✸ How did you spend your free time? Did you play outside or did you sit indoors colouring, reading and daydreaming?

✸ What would you be doing when you lost track of time? What were you good at? Try to remember specific times when this happened.

2. Ask God to remind you of anything you may have forgotten and add it to your notes, and when you've exhausted writing, take a pause!

3. Now review your list and highlight any patterns, or anything which particularly resonates with you, and make a note of any key points here.

YOUR PERSONALITY

'I praise you because I am fearfully and wonderfully made;
your works are wonderful'
(Psalm 139:14).

Read the section on YOUR PERSONALITY in the book.

Make a note of your reflections and thoughts here.

Explore your own personality.

God designed you to His own pattern, not anyone else's. He crafted your personality as an intrinsic part of who you are and how you respond to the world. Your personality is unique to you and is made up of a myriad of qualities and characteristics which make you distinctively you.

It helps to understand your own personality because this gives you clues about the type of work you are suited to. This is only a part of the unique package of GRACE God has for you. He is not limited in how He might use you, regardless of the personality He has gifted you with.

I encourage you to complete the free online personality questionnaire www.16personalities.com[1] which provides a report on your personality across 16 personality factors based on the Myers Briggs Type Indicator personality framework including extroversion and introversion, sensing and intuition, thinking and feeling, judging and perceiving.

ACTIVITY 2:
YOUR PERSONALITY

Purpose

To better understand your personality and the implications this has for your career choices.

Prayer
Father God as I explore my personality, highlight the things
which are important to You which make me the unique person You designed.
In Jesus name, Amen.

Instructions

1. Complete the free online personality questionnaire www.16personalities.com based on the Myers Briggs Type Indicator.

The report on your personality profile generates a lot of information, so I suggest you make a note of anything which particularly resonates with you, which makes you say 'Yes', or which quickens in your spirit or heart. There shouldn't really be any surprises in the results from this questionnaire, but it is helpful to identify the personality traits you have which make you uniquely you!

2. Make a note of your results here.

3. Write your answers to the questions below in the space provided. Consider the things which really resonate with you and also make sense of what you know about yourself.

    ✶   What if anything surprised you?

    ✶   Which aspects of your personality profile really resonate with you?

    ✶   What have you learned about yourself?

❀ What does your personality mean for you in terms of your career choices?

❀ Are there career options you could rule in or rule out? The questionnaire also offers ideas about the types of careers which you might be suited for. I recommend you use these as initial sounding blocks rather than concrete options.

4. Talk about your results with someone you trust. Make a note of the key points from this conversation here.

Remember you are more than a score or a code! You are made up of many different things and your personality is just one part of you. You will be able to see patterns and themes which help uncover your personality, but don't base everything you know about yourself on responses to questionnaires!

YOUR DREAMS

'For God speaks again and again, in dreams, in visions of the night
when deep sleep falls on men as they lie on their beds. He opens their ears
in times like that and gives them wisdom and instruction'
(Job 33:14-16 TLB).

Read the section on YOUR DREAMS in the book.

Make a note of your reflections and thoughts here.

Review your own dreams.

Sometimes God might speak to you in a dream. At other times you might just have dreams about what you would like to do, more like daydreams than dreams you might have when you are asleep. These include dreams about things you always wanted to do! They include dreams God may have planted in you which are waiting to come to fruition.

Your dreams will be entirely personal to you! You may have shared them with some people, or you may have kept them to yourself. God knows your dreams. You may not have had such explicit dreams as Joseph from the Old Testament, as I describe in my book, but it's likely there were dreams you had as a child which held clues as to God's plan for your career, even if you're not doing exactly what you thought you might be doing in your dreams.

We don't stop dreaming when we reach adulthood! Our dreams continue and can impact all aspects of our lives and it's really exciting when we see them realised.

As your dreams rise to the surface in your mind, they are probably worth pursuing, however unrealistic they seem. They will give you clues about your career or the next career steps you will make.

ACTIVITY 3:
WHAT DREAMS HAS GOD GIVEN YOU?

Purpose

To record the dreams God has given you for your career and ponder them with God.

Prayer
Father God remind me of the dreams for my life and career You have given me.
Bring them to mind as I make a note of them now.
In Jesus name, Amen.

Instructions

1. Write down your daydreams using the questions below as a guide.

* What things do you daydream about? (Hint – you might have to go for a walk or take time away from your notebook or computer to really notice what you dream about!) Write down anything which comes to mind and work quickly.

Now focus on specific areas in your life, including your career and see what comes to mind.

Career

Homelife

Family

Friends

Church

Community

2. Write down any night-time dreams

⁕   What do you dream about at night? Make a note of dreams you have had when you were asleep! Write these down as soon as possible after you wake and include as much detail as you can remember.

3. Ponder your dreams with God and see what settles. Go back to the notes you have written and highlight anything that seems significant. Don't worry about how realistic you think they are – 'For nothing is impossible with God' (Luke 1:37)

4. When you have made a note of these dreams you can return to them time and again.

Use this space to record any additional thoughts or insights.

YOUR SPIRITUAL GIFTS

'We have different gifts, according to the grace given to each of us'
(Romans 12:6a).

Read the section on YOUR SPIRITUAL GIFTS in the book.

Make a note of your reflections and thoughts here.

Identify your own spiritual gifts.

Before you begin to explore or review your spiritual gifts, I recommend you pray for discernment, and then take your time! God gives these spiritual gifts, and they can't be boxed up, they can't be compartmentalised in human terms. Identifying spiritual gifts is not an exact science. You can't pick and choose them, but you can ask for them and accept them and then use them in God's service.

Often, spiritual gifts may be given for a season, whereas we mature in others over time. They are like muscles and you need to use them to develop and grow, so it might be you have been given the gift of intercession (praying for other people), but at the moment you are still learning how to intercede for other people.

God doesn't compartmentalise our work and non-work lives and you may find there is an overlap in the spiritual gifts He has given you and where you use them. Things are opened in the heavenly realms which will make a difference in people's lives.

I have created a checklist to help you start to identify or review your own spiritual gifts. As you work through this checklist, I recommend asking Christian friends, colleagues and pastors for their views on what spiritual gifts they think God has given you and why they think you might have these spiritual gifts.

ACTIVITY 4:
YOUR SPIRITUAL GIFTS

Purpose

To review your spiritual gifts and how you use them in your career or at work.

Prayer
Father God thank You for the gifts of Your Holy Spirit, as I pray through
the checklist quicken my heart for the spiritual gifts that are relevant to me.
In Jesus name, Amen.

Instructions

1. Prayerfully complete the Spiritual Gifts Checklist in Appendix One.

2. Highlight your main Spiritual Gifts.

Administration	Apostleship
Craftsmanship	Creative Communication
Discernment	Encouragement
Evangelism	Faith
Giving	Healing
Helps	Hospitality
Interpretation of Tongues	Intercession
Knowledge	Leadership
Mercy	Miracles
Pastor / Shepherd	Prophecy
Service	Teaching
Tongues	Wisdom

3. Reflect on how you use your Spiritual gifts at work.

✿ How do you use these in your career? Write down some specific examples in the table below.

My Main Spiritual Gifts	How I use this gift in my career

4. Discuss your reflections with Christian friends, colleagues and pastors and ask them how they have seen you use your spiritual gifts.

✿ What evidence do they have to suggest a particular gift is true for you? Write your evidence here.

REFLECTION ACTIVITY: YOUR UNIQUE GIFTS

God has gifted you with a unique set of personal gifts which you have unwrapped in this module. Take a moment to review them and reflect on what you have been given.

Purpose

To review all the Gifts God has given you for your career.

Prayer

Father God, thank you for my natural gifts, my personality,

my dreams and the spiritual gifts You have given me.

Help me to use all these for your glory.

In Jesus Name, Amen

Instructions

Reflect on the activities you have completed in this module and write down your reflections here, using the questions as a guide.

Your Natural Gifts

❋ What really resonated with you as you reflected on the things you did as a child?

❋ Make a note of the natural gifts God has given you, the things which come easily to you, and you feel you don't have to try when you are doing this or behaving in a particular way.

Your Personality

✸   How would you describe your personality using one sentence?

✸   Make a note of anything which surprised you about your personality results.

✸   Was there something that really made sense to you which might impact your career or choice of career? Make a note of it here.

Your Dreams

✸   In a sentence or two write down your dreams ... what if I could .... ?

Your Spiritual Gifts

✸   Make a note of your main spiritual gifts.

✸   Consider how you might use these gifts in your career.

2

Gifts
Relationships
Abilities
Curiosities
Experiences

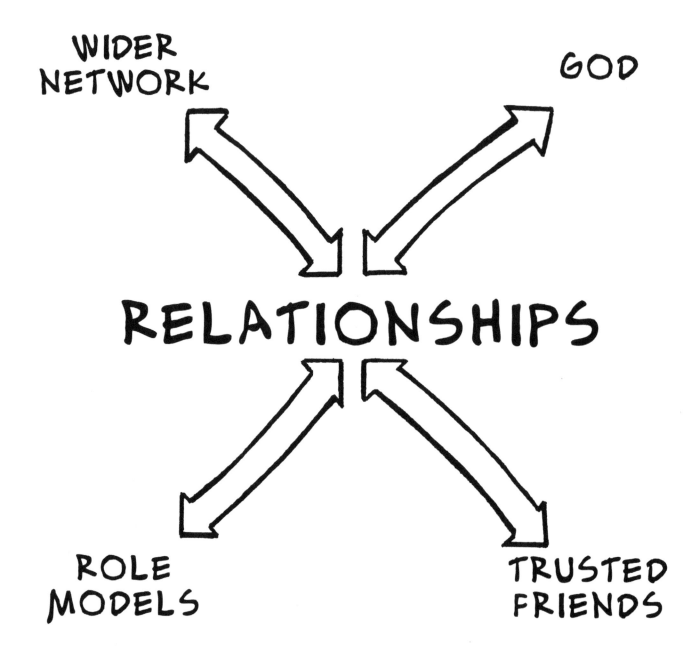

MODULE 2 - RELATIONSHIPS

'I will be a Father to you, and you will be my sons and daughters,
says the Lord Almighty'
(2 Corinthians 6:18).

God Himself exists in loving community in the Trinity, one God in three persons, Father, Son and Holy Spirit. Since we are made in His image (Genesis 1:27), we too are designed to live in loving community with others, as well as with God and He invites us to join in His loving community, as His adopted sons and daughters (Ephesians 1:5).

We are relational beings, and our relationships with other people are essential to our overall wellbeing and sense of purpose. We are connected to many people, some more closely than others, some remotely via social media, and some we see regularly in person.

Your relationships are essential for your career journey, and this module will help you explore those relationships, starting with God. He has a plan for your career, which He will reveal throughout your life, so it makes sense to cultivate Your Relationship with God to find out what He has to say about how you should spend your working life.

God also puts people in our lives as Trusted Friends, the people we are close to and feel able to share our career aspirations and dreams with. Jesus had 12 people to be His disciples, and three of these people He was particularly close to, his close confidants. These people are essential to your career as people who know you really well and can provide trusted advice and guidance.

Beyond this is your Wider Network; the surprising number of people you actually know, all of whom can help in your career, and you can help as well. Then there are Christian Role Models you can learn from, those you know personally, and those in the public eye, or people who have gone before us who can teach us so much from their example.

In this module, take some time now to gather your relationships into one place, in circles of relationship and ask God to clarify your important relationships, recognising they are essential for your career, wellbeing and sense of purpose.

Prayer
Father God thank You for inviting me into a relationship with You.
Thank You for all the significant people You have connected me to. Thank You for
the wider connections You have given me and also for the Christians who have gone ahead
of me who I can draw inspiration from.
In Jesus name, Amen.

Write your own prayer here.

YOUR RELATIONSHIP WITH GOD

"You hem me in, behind and before, and You lay Your hand upon me'
(Psalm 139:5).

Read the section on YOUR RELATIONSHIP WITH GOD in the book.

Make a note of your reflections and thoughts here.

Reflect on your own relationship with God.

Do you want to know God's will and provision for your career? Take the time to get to know Him well and grow your relationship with Him. As the Prodigal Son discovered it's from a deep place of love, acceptance and security that our love for God can flow more freely, from a place of joy rather than duty, a place of ease rather than striving, a place of familial relationship rather than hired hand.

The more you spend time in God's word, the Bible, the more you will understand about what He wants for you. The more time you spend with God praying the more you will learn to hear from Him. The more time you take to listen to Him the more you will recognise His voice! Jesus says, "My sheep listen to my voice; I know them, and they follow me" (John 10:27).

God is not in a hurry, and so in order to hear Him it helps to slow down and take time to hear what He has to say. Find a time and space that suits you best, either a quiet spot at home, or on a daily walk. Take time to ponder with God, ask Him questions and see what comes to mind. You may need to jot these things down when you get back from a walk. Or if you prefer, sit quietly with Him. You could play some worship music and get out your Bible and journal.

ACTIVITY 5:
40 DAYS OF PRAYER FOR YOUR CAREER

Purpose

To spend time over 40 days in prayer with God seeking clarity about your career.

Prayer

Father God – I long to know You more and I pledge to spend more time with You,
through Your word and in prayer, to get to know You and understand the things
that are important to You. Father God thank You for sending Jesus and
the Holy Spirit – search me and know me as I long to know You.
In Jesus Name, Amen

Instructions

1. Choose one Bible passage and one or two specific verses which resonate with you and write them down so you can read them each day.

Here are some Bible passages you could consider

- Parable of the Talents – Matthew 25:14-30
- The Wife of Noble Character – Proverbs 31:10-31
- The Vine and The Branches – John 15:1-17
- A Letter to the Exiles - Jeremiah 29:1-14

And some specific verses

Jeremiah 29:11	Proverbs 3:5-6	Psalm 32:8	Proverbs 16:3
Psalm 37:4	Colossians 3:23-24	Psalm 127:1	Romans 8:28
Matthew 6:33	Matthew 6:34	Matthew 7:7	James 1:5
Proverbs 20:5	Ephesians 2:10	Psalm 139:16b	James 1:17

2. Then write your questions and wait for His answer! Let the questions rest in your heart whilst you write them down. Each time you pray, as things come to mind you think might be from God jot them down and ask for confirmation.

3. When you think you've heard from God, pray for peace.

4. Remember to count off 40 days, so you know where you are, and if you miss a day or two just pick up where you left off!

This is a gentle grace filled process, not something you have to strive at. When you look back at the end of 40 days, you'll be able to see where and how God is at work in your career and how your relationship with Him has deepened as you spend more time with Him.

1. Write your Bible verses here.

2. Write your questions for God here.

3. Write down any answers you think He might give you during the 40 days here.

4. Mark off the 40 days, each day you pray.

1	2	3	4	5	6	7	8	9	10
11	12	13	14	15	16	17	18	19	20
21	22	23	24	25	26	27	28	29	30
31	32	33	34	35	36	37	38	39	40

YOUR TRUSTED FRIENDS

'Plans fail for lack of counsel, but with many advisors they succeed'
(Proverbs 15:22).

Read the section on **YOUR TRUSTED FRIENDS** in the book.

Make a note of your reflections and thoughts here.

Who are your trusted friends?

You are not meant to search for God's purpose for your career in isolation. God puts us in communities where there are people we trust and can confide in.

This could be people in a prayer triplet, where you can be totally honest about your fears and worries as well as being open to their counsel, because they will be listening to God as well as you. Jesus tells us, "For where two or three gather in my name, there am I with them" (Matthew 18:20).

There are also other people, beyond the prayer triplet, who will give you inspiration and support and can help you make decisions about your career. They may not all be Christians, God is not limited to speaking into our lives and careers only through Christians. These are the people you can turn to for advice, and the people you celebrate with in good times and you probably already know who they are.

They are the people you can share your career ideas and considerations with. People who know you well and who you can trust, who encourage and champion you, who help fill you with confidence, who you feel really at ease speaking to. You don't need an invitation to speak with them; there's no agenda, the relationship is natural and there is support and encouragement from people who have your best interests at heart.

These relationships are two-way, give and take, so there are times when they will be supporting you in your career and times when you will be supporting them.

ACTIVITY 6:
YOUR CAREER CHAMPIONS

Purpose

To identify your career champions, give thanks for them and ask God to speak to you through them.

Prayer

Father God – bring to mind the people who should be in my inner circle,
my career champions, the people who know me well. Thank You for these friendships
and help me to be open to anything You want to say through them about my career.
Help me to weigh their words carefully and to seek Your confirmation of them.
In Jesus name, Amen.

Instructions

Take a moment to consider your close relationships, your trusted friends, and write your answers to the questions below.

- Who are your trusted friends? Write down their names.

- Reflect on how often you speak with them – do you need to speak with them more often? Could you arrange a time to meet with them now?

- Write a prayer for each of them by name. Give thanks for them and ask God that they might speak into your life about your career.

YOUR WIDER NETWORK

"Without good direction, people lose their way; the more wise counsel you follow,
the better your chances'
(Proverbs 11:14 MSG).

Read the section on YOUR WIDER NETWORK in the book.

Make a note of your reflections and thoughts here.

Who do you know and where do they work?

As Paul's network was important for his work, so your network is an important element in your career, the people you know and connect with, who in turn connect you with other people. A lot of people shy away from networking but in fact it's really just about relationships and getting to know people.

The world of social media makes this so easy. At the click of a button, you can connect or reconnect with people to keep in touch. However, building good relationships is important and this can take time and requires a bit more than just a click of a button. It's not about what you can get out of a relationship, it's about nurturing relationships, so they become two-way, spending time getting to know people. When these relationships are in place, then God can use them to communicate with you about your career and make connections that can result in career moves and job changes.

Most of us know a lot more people than we realise. Just have a think about who you know from Church, the school gate, your friendship group, societies or clubs you're involved in, your neighbours, any networking groups you belong to. Then consider people you know through your work. Try not to be overwhelmed by volume. This is about quality connections, people you know personally, rather than mere acquaintances.

As you progress through your career journey, consider who is God connecting you with.

ACTIVITY 7:
WHO IS IN YOUR WIDER NETWORK?

Purpose

To identify the people in your wider network, and who God might be connecting you with for this stage of your career.

Prayer

Father God – help me to be aware of the people You are drawing into my wider network, to pay attention to what they say and do, and to ponder this alongside all the other information I am receiving. I pray You would make it abundantly clear what is from You and what is not.

In Jesus name, Amen.

Instructions

1. Create a spidergram of people you know.

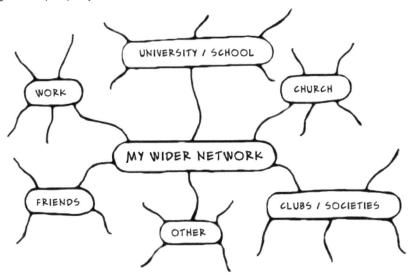

2. Fill it with headings such as work, school, church, clubs, friendships and so on and then list the names of the people you know under this.

3. Quickly write down any names that come to mind, you could use different colour pens to distinguish between different groups.

4. Consider who you know on Facebook, Instagram and other social networks and add specific names. Scroll through prayerfully otherwise your spidergram might grow extra legs!

5. Then go back through the names and jot down the work these people do or their job title if you know it.

6. Review your network on LinkedIn.

- ❋ How up to date is it?
- ❋ Do you need to cull some contacts?
- ❋ Who would you like to connect with professionally?
- ❋ How often do you network with these people? Ask God if there are any people particularly key for this stage of your career.

7. Review your X (Twitter) account

- ❋ Who could you follow and tweet with?

8. Put a + next to people who you know are Christians. God can use anyone to help you explore career options, but with Christians there is an added 'God dimension' to the relationship.

9. Make a note of any specific people you feel God prompting you to contact now and why you think this.

DRAW YOUR SPIDERGRAM HERE.

YOUR ROLE MODELS

'Instruct the wise and they will be wiser still;
teach the righteous and they will add to their learning'
(Proverbs 9:9).

Read the section on **YOUR ROLE MODELS** in the book.

Make a note of your reflections and thoughts here.

Identify your role models.

As well as your wider network you may have people who act as role models for you. These could be people you know from a work setting, from whom you can learn. They might be a manager, or supervisor, or they could be someone who works in a similar industry or sector to you but not actually with you, or people you aspire to be like. A role model is someone who inspires you so much you want to emulate their achievements.

These people are not celebrity role models, and they can come from any walk of life. They are the people who impress you by the work they do, or the people you admire because of the way they behave in their career.

There may be people you don't know personally who can act as a role model for you. You can look to other Christians as trailblazers, aspiring to be more like them. These people are not your idols, they are people you admire and can learn from.

Remember God made each of us to be unique, so although you may admire someone and want to follow their example, you will inevitably do 'it' differently and you'll have different results and outcomes. As Christians we are all the body of Christ, with each of us essential to the full work of building up God's Kingdom (1 Corinthians 12:12-31).

So, go exploring, find out what other Christians are doing in their careers. Follow them on Linked In, Facebook, Instagram or X (Twitter).

ACTIVITY 8: YOUR ROLE MODELS

Purpose

To create a role model collage by choosing the things you admire from different people which impress you. This could be their qualities, their values, their skills or something authentic you notice about them. You can draw inspiration from Christians who are still alive as well as those who have already gone to heaven.

Prayer

Father God, thank You for the role models You have planted in my career, help me to learn from them. Father God also bring to mind Christians from the wider world who I can draw inspiration from for my future career.

In Jesus name, Amen.

Instructions

1. Write down the names of 2 or 3 of your role models.

❋ Who are your role models? Make a note of the people who initially come to mind.

a)

b)

c)

❋ What do you admire most about them?

a)

b)

c)

❋ How could you emulate this in your own career?

2. Choose 1 or 2 well known Christians you admire for the work they do or the impact they have in their sphere of influence. If you're not sure where to start, ask your Christian friends. Who do they know? Who do they follow on social media? Consider people who work in similar areas to you, in your sector, in media, in sport, in business, in politics.

3. Note down their names and commit to researching their careers. Follow them on their social media platforms. What can you learn from their career stories, their successes and failures?

a)

b)

4. List the qualities, skills, or values that you most admire. How do you use these in your career? Write down some specific examples.

* What sets them apart from other people who are not Christians?

* How could you grow in one of these areas in your own career and what difference would this make?

* What small step could you take now?

REFLECTION ACTIVITY: YOUR CIRCLES OF RELATIONSHIPS

Purpose

God made us relational beings, created for connection with Him and also with other people. Relationships are important for your wellbeing and also for your career. It's often obvious who your trusted friends are, the people you can rely on for support and advice. Next there is your wider network and the people God is connecting you to for now and for the future. Then there are your role models, those known to you personally, and those not known personally but who you can learn from by their Christian example.

Prayer
Father God, thank You for fostering relationships, and for Your nurture loving community.
Help me to identify the key relationships around You for my career.
In Jesus name, Amen.

Instructions

1. On the page opposite use the four blank concentric circles for the following exercise.

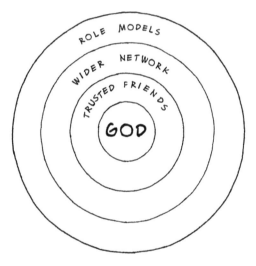

- ❀ Put God in the centre circle.

- ❀ Write the names of your trusted friends in the next circle. This could be a few or up to a dozen.

- ❀ Write the names of key people in your wider network in the third circle. These could be people from church, your work, your wider friendship group, people you know outside of work socially. You can copy them from your spidergram (Activity 7) or start from scratch. You don't need to record them all, just the ones God brings to mind.

- ❀ Make a note of your role models in the fourth circle. You are likely to have between one and three personally known to you.

- ❀ Also make a note of any Christians you don't know personally, but you admire for the work they do that you would like to emulate. You could use a different colour for these people.

2. Then consider the following questions and write down your answers or thoughts.

MY CIRCLES OF RELATIONSHIP

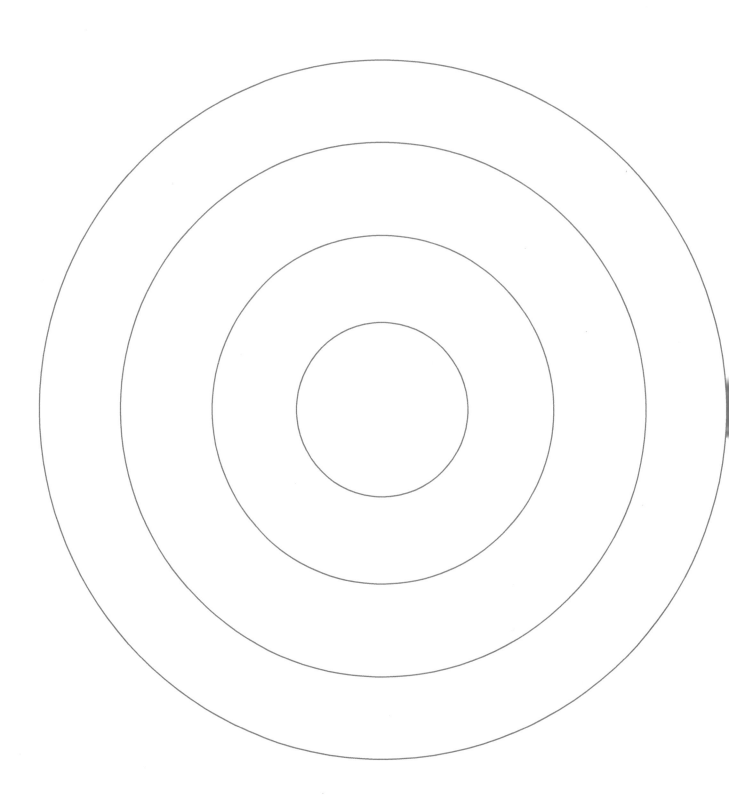

Your Relationship with God.

❀   What could you do to strengthen your relationship with God? Could you spend more time in prayer, reading your Bible, join a fellowship group? Or could you find time to go for a walk with God, and enjoy His creation with Him? What could you commit to? 40 days of Prayer for Your Career or something else?

❀   How will you confirm what you think He is saying to you?

Your Relationship with your Trusted Friends.

❀   What is the quality of your relationship with them?

❀   How do they encourage and champion you?

❀   How much time could you commit to spending with them?

❀　Make a note of anything significant they say about your career?

Your Wider Network.

❀　Who are the people relevant to me?

❀　What is the quality of my relationship with them?

❀　What would I like my relationship with them to be like?

❀　How can I find out more about their work?

Your Role Models.

- What do these people do?

- Why do you admire them?

- What would you like to emulate?

- What could you learn from them?

- How could you use this knowledge in your own career journey?

3

Gifts
Relationships
Abilities
Curiosities
Experiences

MODULE 3 - ABILITIES

'For we are God's handiwork, created in Christ Jesus to do good works,
which God prepared in advance for us to do'
(Ephesians 2:10).

You are God's handiwork. He made you with unique Talents, Skills and Strengths designed specifically to do the work He planned for you. When you find this work, you are walking in God's calling on your life. This is amazing! God loves to reveal Himself to us and, as you explore the abilities He has given you and discover more about yourself you will see God's handiwork in your life.

Over time the natural gifts God has given you grow into talents, skills and strengths which you can use for God's glory. When you're using the abilities God specifically gave you; you will experience fulfilment and satisfaction and you will know you are doing the work God created you for.

In this module, you'll start by reviewing your talents, and then identifying your skills and strengths. This is a process of discovery and revelation and will depend on the stage you have reached in your career and how many years of experience you have gained.

Talents can become skills, and skills can become strengths. However, strengths might also be evident in the way you use a specific skill or how you behave in situations. This is what makes its use unique to you, as you will discover.

Prayer
Father God, thank You for the many abilities You have given me, all the talents,
skills and strengths. As I explore them, I ask Your Holy Spirit to reveal each one to me.
In Jesus name, Amen.

Write your own prayer here.

YOUR TALENTS

'For it will be like a man going on a journey, who called his servants and entrusted
to them his property. To one he gave five talents, to another two, to another one,
to each according to his ability. Then he went away'
(Matthew 25:14-15 ESV).

Read the section on YOUR TALENTS in the book.

Make a note of your reflections and thoughts here.

Identify your own specific talents.

Your talents are specific and unique to you. You were born with them. They are the things which come easily
to you, things you do naturally and the ways in which you naturally respond to situations. This is the overlap
with your natural gifts. Your talents are God given building blocks to be developed and strengthened.

Sometimes your talents are displayed as abilities or skills, and sometimes it's your attitudes, your outlooks,
the way you are kind to people or animals, your love of the outdoors, your passion for books or painting or for
building things.

We can't all enter talent competitions so how do you know what your talents are? God gives us clues. Max
Lucado calls these 'your sweet spot'[1] – times in your near and distant past when you did something well and
enjoyed doing it, and experienced success and satisfaction.

ACTIVITY 9: YOUR TALENT STORIES

Purpose

To identify your God given talents.

Prayer
Father God, thank You for the talents You have given me,
please reveal them to me as I consider what they are.
In Jesus name, Amen.

Instructions

1. Start by reviewing your natural gifts looking for clues for your talents. Review the natural gifts you identified earlier (see Activity 1) and write down key words or phrases that demonstrate a talent.

2. Pray for God to prompt you with reminders of stories which illustrate your talents.

3. Recall 2 or 3 times when you were totally absorbed in something as a child. Try to think of specific examples or occasions where you were totally absorbed. This should be a specific event, not a generalised activity. Make a brief note of them here.

51

4. Next tell the story of what happened in each specific occasion or example. Write these stories, you can use bullet points if you prefer. Describe what happened in as much detail as you can remember. The more detail you can remember the better. You can use the following questions as a prompt, but don't just answer the questions – tell your story in your own words!

- What happened?
- What were you doing?
- Who was there?
- What was the occasion?
- What did you specifically enjoy?
- How did you feel?
- How do you know you were absorbed?
- What was the result or outcome which you found so satisfying?

WRITE YOUR CHILDHOOD TALENT STORIES HERE.

CONTINUE TO WRITE YOUR CHILDHOOD TALENT STORIES HERE.

5. Now it's time to look for clues! Go back over what you have written with a highlighter and mark any words which really resonate with you, whether they are verbs, nouns, environments, or feelings.

6. Make a note of any patterns or repetitions.

7. When you spot a talent use a few words or a sentence or two to describe what this talent is.

Sometimes talents lie dormant and are not fully realised until we are adults. Try this exercise again for a time when you were totally absorbed in something as an adult. These can be examples from any area of your life, work or non-work related. Remember, each example should be a specific event, not a generalised activity. Use as much detail as you can remember to flesh out your story using the questions as a guide.

WRITE YOUR ADULT TALENT STORIES HERE.

CONTINUE TO WRITE YOUR ADULT TALENT STORIES HERE.

YOUR SKILLS

'Also I have given ability to all the skilled workers to make everything
I have commanded you'
(Exodus 31:6b).

Read the section on YOUR SKILLS in the book.

Make a note of your reflections and thoughts here.

What skills are you good at?

Skills are abilities you use to accomplish a task. They are very much about getting things done, which have an end result, often without realising you are using skills. Skills can be learned and improved through repetition. Many are also transferable. The challenge is knowing what your skills are, describing them to others and knowing the ones you want to use or develop in the future.

There is so much you can do when you know what your skills are. You can improve them and grow them, you can learn new ones, you can stop using those you're not particularly good at. It's really well worth taking time to explore your skills, asking God what He thinks, and then talking to one of your trusted friends about what they think your skills are. Which ones are your core skills, lesser skills, enjoyable skills, transferable skills?

In the world of work, there are many skills and many skill mixes and levels of proficiency. These skills fall into different categories such as creative, practical, technical, people related, processing, leadership, and personal. Some skills are specifically related to a particular career sphere and others are transferable. It can be quite a challenge to identify your skills, so I recommend a multi-layered approach.

Remember, you use skills in all aspects of your life and sometimes it's helpful to explore the skills you use outside of your current career, in voluntary roles, leisure activities or even in your homelife.

ACTIVITY 10: CREATE YOUR SKILLS BANK

Purpose

To identify and rank your key skills.

Start with some prayer! Identifying your skills can be a big task so ask God to go before you to reveal the skills He wants.

Prayer
Father God, thank You for the many skills You have blessed me with. Please prompt my thoughts as I consider my skills and how I might use them and grow them for Your glory.
In Jesus name, Amen.

Instructions

As you compile your list of skills, let God speak to you about the ones He wants you to use.

Pray about your skills and notice which ones make your heart quicken, which ones seem appealing to you.

Take a stack of post-it notes and some pens and use them to jot down skills as you think of them to help you create your skills bank.

1. Consider your current role.

- What are the skills you use each day? Jot them down on the post-it notes as they come to mind.

2. Make a note of any activities, jobs or volunteering you may do or have done outside paid employment.

- What skills were you using for each role? Jot these down on post-it notes.

3. Consider the skills you've used in the past, both work and non-work related. Write these on post-it notes as well.

4. Organise these skills into groups under headings such as Creative or People or Personal or Technical skills. Consider ones which go naturally together.

- Are there some skills you don't want to use any more? Cast them aside.

5. Then rank your skills in order of proficiency.

- How good are you at this skill? Use grades A B C D E to help you.

List your key skills from this activity on the next page.

LIST YOUR KEY SKILLS HERE

LIST YOUR KEY SKILLS HERE

6. Now choose the ones you want to use more in the future. Highlight them.

❋   How could you grow and develop these skills? Write your thoughts here.

7. Talk this through with someone you trust, so you don't get overwhelmed.

You now have a big 'bank' of skills which you can draw upon. Some will excite you; some might surprise you; all will be useful for your work and career.

8. God also fills His people with His Spirit for the workplace so that when they use their skills, other people are impacted beyond our expectations. Remember Bezalel; he was filled with the Spirit of God as well as being a skilled craftsman. God says, "I've filled him with the Spirit of God, giving him skill and know-how and expertise in every kind of craft to create designs .... he's an all-round craftsman" (Exodus 31:3 MSG).

So even when you think you might not be particularly skilled at something God can use you and grow and develop this skill for His glory.

❋   How might the Holy Spirit be using the skills He's given you above and beyond your expectations?

9. Ponder your list for a few days and then go back to review your skills bank.

❋   Do you feel the same prompting?

❋   Make a note of any changes/updates to your skills bank.

YOUR STRENGTHS

'The joy of the Lord is your strength'
(Nehemiah 8:10b).

Read the section on YOUR STRENGTHS in the book.

Make a note of your reflections and thoughts here.

Reveal your own strengths.

A strength begins with a talent. As you grow your talents with time, learning, knowledge and practice they become strengths. Sometimes your strengths grow from specific skills; and at other times your strengths come from specific characteristics unique to you; the way you 'do' things, the innate part of who you are and how you behave, such as kindness or courage or sensitivity.

I recommend using Strengths Profile[2] online assessment which provides you with a personal profile based on your performance, energy and use of your strengths, across four quadrants including,

Realised Strengths – strengths you use and enjoy to help you flourish.

Learned Behaviours – things you've learned to do well but may not enjoy and drain your energy.

Weaknesses – things you find hard and don't enjoy.

Unrealised Strengths – strengths you don't use as often but would really benefit from using more to gain more energy and fulfilment – these are your hidden talents!

Your answers to the online questionnaire are likely to be reliant on your current situation. There are 60 strengths defined in the Strengths Profile and you can find them listed, along with their definitions, in Appendix Two. The report from the online assessment will highlight those most key at this moment in time.

ACTIVITY II:
COMPLETE YOUR STRENGTHS PROFILE

Purpose

To complete your own Strengths Profile and understand the strengths which will energise you and those you could use to help you flourish in your career.

Prayer
Father God, thank You for the talents you gave me which have grown into strengths which energise me and help me flourish. Help me to develop the unrealised strengths, the hidden talents You have gifted me with.
In Jesus Name, Amen.

Instructions

1. Complete your own Free Starter Profile at www.strengthsprofile.com.

You will be asked to set up an account and then taken through the online questionnaire which will take you about 20 minutes to answer. For each question go with your gut answer rather than over thinking your answer. You will receive your own personal profile via email. If you want to upgrade your profile you can pay for the Introductory Profile which will give you further information on your strengths, including your top 7 realised strengths, your top 7 unrealised strengths, 4 learned behaviours, 3 weaknesses and action advice to release your potential using your unrealised strengths and access to an interactive Goals Planner and possible career areas.

2. Make a note of your Strengths here.

Realised Strengths	Unrealised Strengths
Learned Behaviours	Weaknesses

3. Then answer the following questions.

YOUR REALISED STRENGTHS

✺ What resonates with you about your realised strengths?

✺ Which are you most proud of?

✺ Which would you like to be known for?

✺ Which are serving you best in your current role?

✺ How might you use a combination of your realised strengths in a way that is unique to you?

YOUR LEARNED BEHAVIOURS

❀ How do you feel about your learned behaviours?

❀ Is there one you are using too much which you need to stop using?

❀ How reliant are you on your learned behaviours in your current role?

❀ What action could you take to become less reliant?

❀ Are you relying on any learned behaviours which are draining your energy?

YOUR WEAKNESSES

❋ How are you going to stop using your weaknesses, the things which drain you of energy?

❋ Which strengths in the other three quadrants you could use instead?

YOUR UNREALISED STRENGTHS

❋ Which unrealised strength would you like to dial up?

❋ What one way could you increase your usage of your unrealised strengths to boost your energy in your career?

❋ Which of your unrealised strengths could you develop by using it more? How might you do this?

YOUR SUPER STRENGTH

🌸 How could you combine your realised strengths with your unrealised strengths to promote their use?

REFLECTION ACTIVITY: YOUR GOLDEN THREADS

Purpose

God gifted us uniquely with talents, skills and strengths and He wants us to use them. During your exploration, you will have found there are themes and ideas that are repeated, threads connecting your talents, skills and strengths. I like to call them "golden threads." This is where you can see the talents God "knitted together" in you have developed and grown into skills and then strengths. You will also have an idea of the skills and strengths you want to build on for the future.

Prayer

Father God, thank You for all the abilities You have given me. Help me to use the talents, skills and strengths You have given me and help me to develop and grow the ones
I need for my future career.
In Jesus name, Amen.

Instructions

Take some time to reflect on the Abilities God has given you and answer the questions below.

Review Your Talent Stories

- ❋ What are your key talents? Jot down single words or a sentence or two here to act as a reminder.

Consider Your Skills Bank

- ❋ What are your top 5 skills – the skills you are most proficient in?

- ❋ Which skills do you not want to use any more?

✳ Which skills do you want to use more?

✳ What skills do you want to develop or learn?

✳ How do you feel God prompting you to use your skills through the power of His Holy Spirit?

Reflect on Your Strengths

✳ What are your key strengths? How could you use them more?

✳ Which learned behaviours are you going to rely on less so you feel less drained?

✳ What will you do instead of using your weaknesses?

✳ How will you use your unrealised strengths, your hidden talents more?

✳ What do you think God might be saying to you about your talents, skills and strengths?

4

Gifts
Relationships
Abilities
Curiosities
Experiences

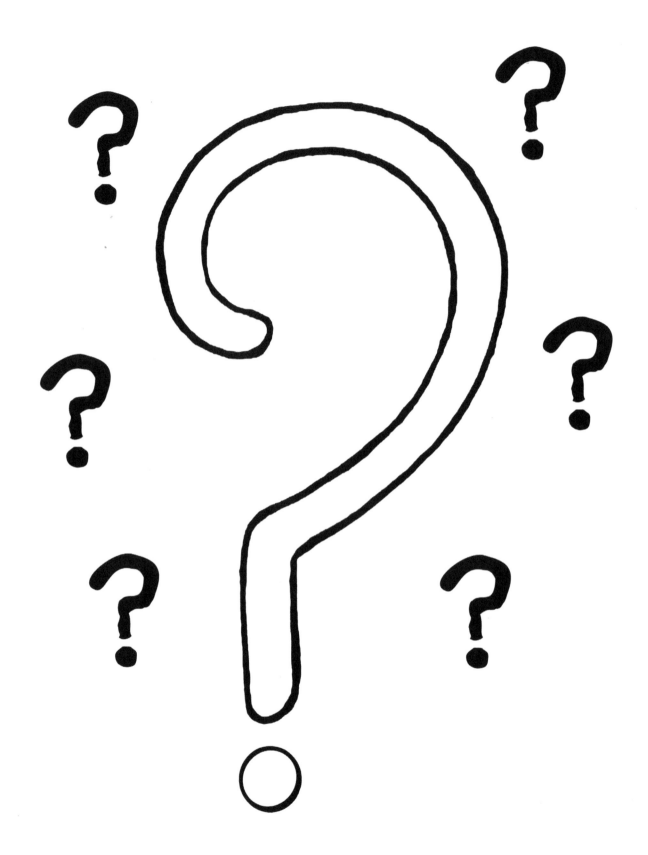

MODULE 4 - CURIOSITIES

'Through Him all things were made; without Him nothing
was made that has been made'
(John 1:3).

God's creation is awesome and there is so much for us to learn. He has hidden things for us to find and He reveals things to us all the time. The things you are curious about give you clues about what He might be hiding for you to find. You might discover it in:

Your Education - the subjects you chose to study.

Your Knowledge - gained through living life.

Your Interests - the topics in which you are keenly interested.

Your Compassions - the causes you care deeply about.

Your Inner Wisdom - the things you feel God has put on your heart.

Your Revelations from God - the ideas He has revealed to you through His word, prophecies or other people.

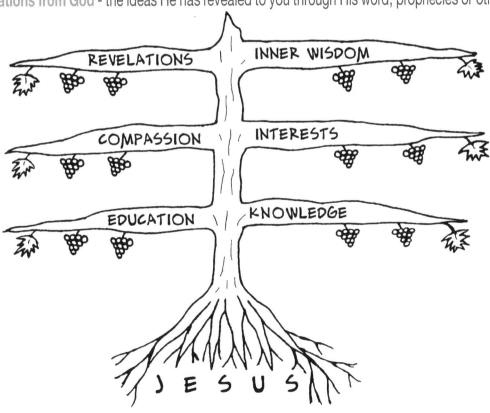

Your Vine of Curiosity will be personal to you and it may take time to develop as you consider each of the different sections or branches. You may find some are particularly clear to you whilst others take more discernment and prayer. God is not in a rush, so take your time as you let your curiosity grow in your vine.

This module will help you explore how your curiosities could lead to career ideas. Each section will focus on a different branch, one for your Education, your Knowledge, your Interests, your Compassions (things you care about), your Inner Wisdom (things buried deep in your heart) and your Revelations from God. There are suggested activities to help you flesh out your thoughts in each area before you decide what will go on your Vine.

At the end of the module there are instructions provided so you can create your Vine of Curiosity, where you will prune (John 15:1-2) your ideas and then populate your own Vine.

Prayer

Father God, thank You for the curiosity You have given me. Please prompt me as I consider the things I am curious about. Help me to discard the things which are not from You and take note of the things which are from You.

In Jesus name Amen.

Write your own prayer here.

YOUR EDUCATION

'Above all and before all, do this: Get Wisdom!
Write this at the top of your list: Get Understanding!'
(Proverbs 4:7 MSG).

Read the section on YOUR EDUCATION in the book.

Make a note of your reflections and thoughts here.

Record key aspects of your education.

God uses people who are fully educated as well as those who are not. He is not limited by what you did or didn't learn at school. In His eyes your education is much broader. Often, He will use people before they are fully trained or educated.

Your education may have directly led you to a specific career, as your schooling led from one thing to another chronologically and you built up qualifications step by step. Or your education may not have set you up for your career aspirations at all. There will have been choices you had to make along the way which will have impacted each stage of your education. This is not just about the subjects you studied, but what you actually learnt and enjoyed.

When you consider your education include both what you learnt in school and any formal education you had post school. Also think about the things you learnt outside of school. Were you involved in sport or music or drama or scouts or martial arts? Think in terms of topics of what you learned from your education and focus on the things you enjoyed or found useful.

Remember you're looking for clues about God's plan for your career. Often these clues are best found in the subjects you made an active decision to learn about, so this would include the subjects you specifically chose to study rather than those you were forced to study.

ACTIVITY 12: YOUR EDUCATION BRANCH

Purpose

To record the key elements of your education which could impact your career choices.

Prayer
Father God, thank You for my education. As I review it now to plot out
my Education branch remind me of anything I may have forgotten which
is of relevance to me for my future career.
In Jesus name, Amen.

Instructions

1. Make a note of anything of relevance about your education – these should be things you really enjoyed learning.

2. Note down your specific qualifications.

⚜   What other things did you learn outside of your formal education?

✳   What grades or levels did you achieve in these areas?

✳   Was there anything specific you learnt relevant to your career?

3. Go back over your list and highlight or put a star against anything you enjoyed learning the most.

YOUR KNOWLEDGE

'The heart of the discerning acquires knowledge, for the ears of the wise seek it out'
(Proverbs 18:15).

Read the section on YOUR KNOWLEDGE in the book.

Make a note of your reflections and thoughts here.

Explore your personal knowledge.

God uses the knowledge we gain throughout our lives. In James 3:17 it says, 'the wisdom that comes from heaven is first of all pure; then peace-loving, considerate, submissive, full of mercy and good fruit, impartial and sincere'. We all have specific ways of interacting with knowledge, so it is not just what we know, but how we use what we know.

Howard Gardener, a psychologist, developed a theory of Multiple Intelligences[1] suggesting that humans have a number of discrete intellectual capacities. He identified 8 different components of Multiple Intelligence - Bodily/Kinaesthetic, Musical, Logical/Mathematical, Interpersonal, Intra-personal, Linguistic, Spatial/Visual, Naturalistic.

Using Gardner's Intelligences provides a very useful framework for sorting your knowledge, because it is intelligence driven rather than subject driven and helps you think about the knowledge you've gained in a broader context. When you think about your knowledge, consider what you've learned from work, the courses you've attended and what you gained 'on-the-job'. Also consider what knowledge you learned outside work, through volunteering or unpaid work, or just being curious about the world we live in.

As far as possible try to be circumspect and just note down key things. You can always take a highlighter to the ones which appeal to you most to explore them in more depth later on. For now, it is about being clear about your areas of knowledge, focusing on your expertise, the knowledge which you are known for.

ACTIVITY 13:
YOUR KNOWLEDGE BRANCH

Purpose

To identify your key areas of knowledge and determine which ones could provide clues for your future career.

Prayer
Father God, thank You for all the knowledge You have given me.
Please bring to mind anything You want me to add to my Knowledge branch at this time.
In Jesus Name, Amen.

Instructions

* Which of Gardner's Intelligences resonate with you the most?

1. List them in order of preference based on what you know about yourself.

2. Reflect on other knowledge you have learned from work, courses attended and things you know from outside work. Note these down under the relevant intelligences.

YOUR KNOWLEDGE

- ❀ Bodily/Kinaesthetic

- ❀ Musical

- ❀ Logical/Mathematical

- ❀ Interpersonal

- ❀ Intra-personal

- ❀ Linguistic

- ❀ Spatial/Visual

- ❀ Naturalistic

YOUR INTERESTS

'And now, dear brothers and sisters, one final thing. Fix your thoughts on what is true,
and honourable, and right, and pure, and lovely, and admirable. Think about things
that are excellent and worthy of praise'
(Philippians 4:8 NLT).

Read the section on YOUR INTERESTS in the book.

Make a note of your reflections and thoughts here.

What are your interests?

God has made a vast universe, a beautiful world with so much to be discovered. There is much to be curious about. He has made each of us with unique interests and curiosities. It's exciting to be able to explore the things which interest you. This is the time to let your mind wander, to let your thoughts flow!

Being interested in the work you do makes a huge difference to your daily wellbeing. It could be you're interested in people and your work fulfils this interest or it could be you're fascinated by how our bodies work, or you love animals, or you're interested in patterns, music, or the outdoors. When you know what your interests are and can talk about them enthusiastically this will help bring alive a job application or help you come across as passionate and authentic in an interview.

Think through your day or week. What has stopped you in your tracks; what has distracted you, the topics you find yourself exploring or talking about? These could be at work or outside work. They could be full-blown hobbies or just small things which consistently attract your attention.

Think about what type of magazine you would pull off a rack whilst waiting for a train, or what YouTube videos you find yourself continually watching, or the podcasts you regularly tune into, or the TV programmes you tend to watch. What do you do when you have a moment to yourself?

ACTIVITY 14:
YOUR INTERESTS BRANCH

Purpose

To consider all your interests and identify those that are significant for your career choices.

Prayer
Father God, thank You so much for the many things which interest me.
Give me discernment as I explore them on my Interest branch.
In Jesus name, Amen.

Instructions

1. Review your answers to the questions below and write down key words on yellow stickies or cards. Don't worry about focussing on details at this moment, you're looking for clues which you can come back to later.

Let your mind flow! Use these questions to guide you.

- ❀ What interests you outside work?
- ❀ What are you curious about? These could be things you've dipped you toe in the water with, or you are saving to do later, but haven't quite got round to.
- ❀ What topics are you drawn to on television, or in the news, or in social media?
- ❀ What leisure things do you enjoy doing? Sport, cooking, shopping, gardening …?
- ❀ What would you happily spend hours pursuing or learning about?

2. Organise your interests under relevant themes, either using the Holland Occupational Themes[2] or using your own headings.

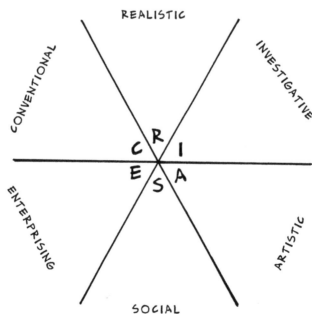

3. Put to one side anything you consider a hobby, or a 'love to do' but you wouldn't want to do as a job.

LIST YOUR INTERESTS HERE

4. Rank your interests depending on what is most appealing to you using a scale of 1-5, where 1 is not appealing and 5 is really appealing.

5. What, if anything, do you think God is saying about your career choices from the clues your interests have given you?

YOUR COMPASSION

'The Lord is gracious and compassionate, slow to anger and rich in love.
The Lord is good to all; He has compassion on all He has made'
(Psalm 145:8-9).

Read the section on YOUR COMPASSION in the book.

Make a note of your reflections and thoughts here.

What moves your compassion?

Compassion is when you are moved enough by something to take action, to want to make a difference.

Sometimes when we look around us, or read or watch the news, we can be overwhelmed by the needs of our world. Just as God has made each of us different and unique, so He has given each of us a bit of His creation, earthly and spiritual, to care deeply about. These are the things you ache to do something to help. It could be people who are lost, single mothers, homelessness, persecuted Christians, debt, people in prison, slavery, trafficked people, mental health, the voiceless, the broken, the planet.

Passion can also be a powerful indicator of your compassions. It can be related to your emotions and also your interests. Some things on your list of interests could be things you are passionate about. Your passions can drive your compassions!

There are so many 'causes' in the world that sometimes understanding which ones tug on your heart can be a bit overwhelming, so start small. Ask God to remind you of the time you felt sad about a homeless person, or when your heart went out to a single mother who was struggling in the local supermarket, or when you felt angry about the way refugees are treated, or your feelings of frustration about the way our planet is being abused. These are the things which can give you clues about your compassions.

ACTIVITY 15:
YOUR COMPASSION BRANCH

Purpose

To identify your compassions and understand the ones God wants you to act upon.

Prayer
Father God, I know Your heart beats with compassion. Fill my heart with Your compassion and let Your Holy Spirit guide me as I list the things which fill me with passion and compassion. In Jesus name, Amen.

Instructions

1. Prayerfully ask God to reveal to you everything which caused compassion to rise up in you. You can use these questions as a guide.

* What are the things you care about, the things which move you?

* When you look at the world around you what touches you?

* What causes a lurch in your heart?

* What are the things you long to change?

✺ What do you feel passionate about?

✺ What are the needs you have been most responsive to in the past?

✺ What are the causes you are already involved in?

✺ Are you volunteering in areas you feel passionate about already?

2. List your ideas as a stream of consciousness on the next page.

3. Keep writing until you run out of ideas.

4. Take a break.

5. Go back over your list and grade them according to how compassionate, or passionate you feel.

Use grade ...

A - for things you feel really compassionate about, things you find dwell in your mind.

B - for things you feel moderately compassionate about.

C - for things which move you but don't cause you sleepless nights.

You may find there are some things you want to grade A*

LIST YOUR COMPASSIONS

6. Make a note here of any actions you feel God wants you to take, or how God might be stirring your compassions for you to use in your career.

YOUR INNER WISDOM

'Yet you desired faithfulness even in the womb,
you taught me wisdom in that secret place'
(Psalm 51:6).

Read the section on YOUR INNER WISDOM in the book.

Make a note of your reflections and thoughts here.

What is your inner wisdom telling you?

Your inner wisdom is the personal knowledge stored in the secret part of you, the things you know about yourself which are hidden in your heart. They are not necessarily the things you know about yourself in your head, and are not the same as your intuition, or your compassion, or your inner voice. This is more about the things you 'know' you are meant to do in your life or your career, the things you feel 'in your gut' which you were meant to do in your lifetime. These are things planted deep in you which God is longing to help you unearth. When He was creating your inmost being, He planted these ideas in you, ready for you to act on them. These things are different for all of us.

This might need some discernment and prayer! You might need to ask God specifically if there is anything He wants you to put on this branch.

ACTIVITY 16:
WHAT IS IN YOUR INNER WISDOM?

Purpose

To bring your inner wisdom into the light.

Prayer
Father God, thank You for the things You planted in my inner wisdom as You knit
me together in my mothers' womb. Prompt me now as I write them down.
In Jesus Name, Amen.

Instructions

1. Start with prayer – ask God to reveal what He has planted in your inner wisdom, when He knit you together in your mother's womb.

2. Then write these things down – you should feel a surge of recognition or excitement, small or large, a sense of 'rightness' as you write! Don't worry if your list is short, it is the content which is of value not the quantity.

3. Ask God if there are any actions you need to take to act on your inner wisdom

4. Make a note of His answers here.

YOUR REVELATIONS FROM GOD

'If people can't see what God is doing, they stumble all over themselves;
But when they attend to what He reveals, they are most blessed'
(Proverbs 29:18 MSG).

Read the section on YOUR REVELATIONS FROM GOD in the book.

Make a note of your initial thoughts here.

What has God revealed to you?

God's revelations about your career will be very personal and specific. They may include specific prophecies spoken over you; Bible verses which are significant for you; words of wisdom from other Christians; suggestions which come from personal prayer times; ideas sparked by exploring God's amazing creation.

Revelation can be the light bulb moment when you're reading your Bible and suddenly something 'clicks' and you understand what the passage is about. It feels special and significant as if God is speaking directly to you. It's when God deepens your understanding by revealing the Scriptures to you through the Holy Spirit in a way which is deeply personal to you. Or God may reveal Himself through creation, and you may find things make sense to you through nature, when a spiritual truth becomes apparent through a physical example, or through a conversation with someone, or even through circumstances which may appear co-incidental but are in fact God speaking to you.

There might be specific Bible verses He has given you. There might be words of wisdom given to you from another believer, through the Holy Spirit. You might have had word of prophecy given to you. My advice here is to rest in God and see what He brings to mind! Take your time over this and be prepared to come back to it a few times.

ACTIVITY 17:
YOUR REVELATIONS FROM GOD

Purpose

To record the revelations God has given you for your career.

Prayer
Father God, thank You for the things You have revealed to me about my career.
Bring them to mind again now.
In Jesus Name, Amen.

Instructions

Start with prayer and ask God to remind you of things He has specifically revealed to you.

* Are there specific Bible verses or passages that God has revealed to you? Write them here.

* Are there things another believer said to you which touched you deeply? List them here.

* Have you had words of prophecy prayed over you? What were they? Write them here.

* Are there particular events or circumstances where God has revealed things to you?

REFLECTION ACTIVITY:
YOUR VINE OF CURIOSITY

'I am the true vine, and my Father is the gardener. He cuts off every branch
in me that bears no fruit, while every branch that does bear fruit He prunes so
that it will be even more fruitful'
(John 15:1-2).

Purpose

Throughout this chapter you will have gathered lots of ideas of the things you are curious about. Now it is time to create your own Vine of Curiosity by going back through each area prayerfully pruning so you are left with something manageable.

Prayer

Father God, thank You for the curiosity You have given me. Prompt me and remind me of things relevant to me for each of the branches as I create my Vine of Curiosity.
In Jesus name, Amen.

Instructions

1. Go back over the previous activities in this section and use a highlighter or sticky labels to prayerfully mark the key things which stand out for you.

You could use the following scale to help your pruning process.

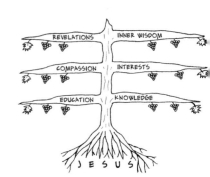

- ❋ **A** - This is really important for me, I'm really drawn to it.

- ❋ **B** - This is somewhat important for me.

- ❋ **C** - I'm interested but don't feel prompted to take it further.

- ❋ **D** - This is part of who I am but it is time to let this go.

2. Then draw your own Vine of Curiosity on the opposite page. Write JESUS at the bottom of the page where the roots of the Vine would be.

3. Next draw branches for each different area; education, knowledge, interests, compassion, inner wisdom and revelation.

4. Then populate the drawing with words or pictures that you have highlighted or starred as you complete each branch. You could use different coloured pens for each branch to help make your Vine more dynamic. Don't be surprised if some branches have more on them than others.

5. Take a break! Let this settle for a day or two.

6. Then as you review what you've done, add any additional items, as God prompts you.

DRAW YOUR VINE OF CURIOSITY HERE

5

Gifts
Relationships
Abilities
Curiosities
Experiences

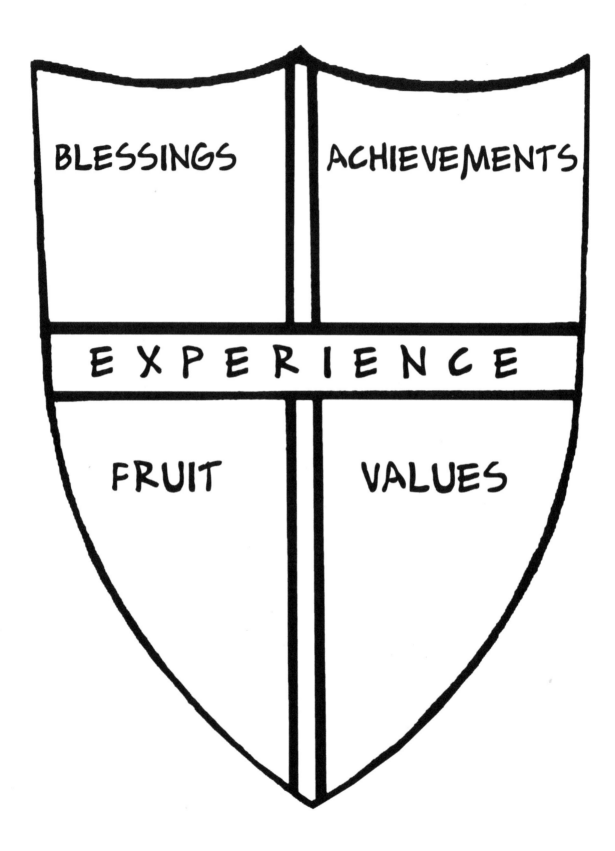

MODULE 5 - EXPERIENCES

'And we know that in all things God works for the good of those who love Him,
who have been called according to His purpose'
(Romans 8:28).

Hindsight is a wonderful thing. Søren Kierkegaard, the Christian philosopher wrote "Life can only be understood backwards; but it must be lived forwards." (Volume IV of his journals, written around 1843). Kierkegaard suggests we can only really understand our lives by looking back on things we've already done.

When you look back you can see the clues God has given you for your future and unearth the treasure He has left to guide you on your Career Journey. We all have stories from our career journeys that will impact on what we do next, but it's knowing where to look. The Message version of Galatians 6:4-5 says, 'Make a careful exploration of who you are and the work you have been given, and then sink yourself into that. Don't be impressed with yourself. Don't compare yourself with others. Each of you must take responsibility for doing the creative best you can with your own life'.

As you begin this careful exploration of your career firstly look at the big picture and review your Career Journey to date. Then you can focus on your Achievements, the satisfying times as well as the difficult times when you had to dig deep to overcome them and the lessons you learned. Armed with these stories you will be able to identify the Fruit in your career. The idea of bearing fruit in your career encompasses not just what you do or have done, but also how you do it and how your character displays spiritual fruit. You will also consider the Blessings God has provided in your career, helping you to lift your gaze to Him and identify how He is at work in and through your career. Finally, you will uncover the Values that are unique to you. Knowing, understanding and articulating your values is arguably the most important aspect of flourishing in your career because it is how you feel most authentic and true to yourself and who God has made you to be.

Prayer
Father God, as I explore my experiences, both in life and work,
help me reflect on the themes and lessons You want me to take forward.
In Jesus name, Amen.

Write your own prayer here.

YOUR CAREER JOURNEY

'Like an open book, You watched me grow from conception to birth;
all the stages of my life were spread out before You.
The days of my life all prepared before I'd even lived one day'
(Psalm 139:15-16 MSG).

Read the section on YOUR CAREER JOURNEY in the book.

Make a note of your reflections and thoughts here.

Plot your own career journey.

You can learn so much about your character, skills, values, strengths and career motivations by reviewing your career journey. There are always highs and lows, peaks and troughs, times of change, questionable decisions, times of learning and possibly times of waiting.

As you think about your own career journey start by considering the big picture. What does your career journey look like? Is it an upward curve, a downward trajectory, is it hilly or mountainous with highs and lows? What were the causes of highs, lows and stable times? What skills have you picked up along the way? How did you make decisions about turning points? What life events impacted your career? You might need to make a list of things before you plot them on your own timeline.

If your career is short, focus on your childhood experiences. If it's longer, then focus on the major changes, the things that had the most impact for you. You may need to include personal circumstances on your timeline because things that happen in our personal lives can have a significant impact on our careers and working lives. This is all part of life's rich tapestry, whether good or bad.

Next mark on your timeline times when you felt close to Jesus, times when He felt further away and why was this? What was it about those times that made you feel close to or far away from God and how did you know? Where was Jesus in the stressful times? Where was He in your successful times? Make a note of any themes you notice. It's fascinating to see where Jesus is making an impact in your career. Can you identify any golden threads?

ACTIVITY 18:
YOUR CAREER JOURNEY

Purpose

To plot your career journey reviewing the highs and lows, turning points, and career experiences that have shaped you.

Prayer
Father God, as I draw my career journey, remind me of significant experiences
that are preparing me for what comes next.
In Jesus name, Amen.

Instructions

1. Using the template provided, write your current age at the right-hand end of the line, and then mark off relevant intervals going backwards in time until your birth at the left-hand end of the line. The picture you will draw of your career journey will include highs and lows joined together going across the page.

2. Note any significant positive experiences above the line, placing them higher up the page the more positive they are.

3. Note any significant negative experiences below the line, again marking them lower down the page the more negative they were.

4. You might find you need to write a list of all these things before committing them to your timeline.

5. Connect each significant event, positive or negative, to represent your career journey.

6. Now mark on your timeline, in a new colour – times when you felt close to Jesus, times when He felt further away.

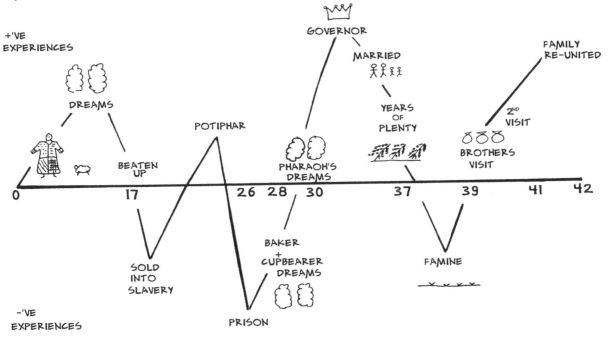

YOUR CAREER JOURNEY

7. Talk this through with someone you trust, using the reflective questions below

✤   What were the causes of highs, lows, stable times?

✤   What skills have you picked up along the way?

✤   How did you make decisions about turning points?

✤   What life events impacted your career?

✤   What was it about the times that made you feel close or far away from God and how did you know?

✤   Where was Jesus in the stressful times and successful times?

8. Make a note of any themes you notice, the major turning points, how you coped with negative experiences, any lessons learned, and anything you feel God is saying to you about your career journey.

YOUR ACHIEVEMENTS

'My son do not forget my teaching, but let your heart keep my commandments,
for length of days and years of life and peace they will add to you. Let not steadfast love
and faithfulness forsake you; bind them around your neck; write them on the tablet
of your heart. So, you will find favour and good success in the sight of God and man'
(Proverbs 3:1-4 ESV).

Read the section on YOUR ACHIEVEMENTS in the book.

Make a note of your reflections and thoughts here.

Describing your satisfying achievements.

We live in a society that values achievement; our CVs include details of our achievements and we are asked in job interviews about our successes and achievements. The definition of achievement is "a thing done successfully with effort, skill, or courage"[1]. Your past achievements can give you clues about your skills and strengths for the future. They are great places to glean the gifts God has given us.

Think about your achievements in two ways. Firstly, the achievements you have found most satisfying and secondly, the achievements when you've had to overcome difficulties and obstacles. It is often said that we learn more from adversity and mistakes than from when things are going well.

The STAR story-telling method is a great way of capturing the key elements of satisfying achievements. Briefly describe the Situation, then the Task. Then describe the Actions you took and state the Results. This way you can capture what happened and what you gained so that you can easily explain this to other people.

ACTIVITY 19:
YOUR STAR ACHIEVEMENTS

Purpose

To identify key career achievements and describe them using the STAR framework.

Prayer

Father God, thank You for my career achievements. Bring to mind those
you want me to focus on and Holy Spirit guide me as I tell these stories now.
In Jesus name, Amen.

Instructions

1. List the achievements you are most proud of. Try to make sure you have at least 5.

Flesh out each achievement using the STAR story telling method and write these in the boxes provided.

- Describe the Situation.

  Provide the context. This should be a specific event, rather than a generalised description. Note down key details about the context.

- Note the Task, or the goal.

  This should be the specific goal you wanted to achieve, or the task that needed to be completed.

- Describe the Actions you took.

  List the specific steps you took to achieve your task. Describe them in as much detail as you can. You might need to review them to see if any are left off.

- State the Results.

  Again, be specific and explain what the outcome was and your role in this. Explain what you accomplished and use facts and figures where possible rather than generalisations. Make a note of why you were proud of this result and what you found satisfying about this achievement.

Star One	Description
Situation What was the situation? What problem did you need to solve? What was the context?	
Task What was your specific task? What did you set out to achieve?	
Action What did you do? What steps did you take to solve the problem? What improvements did you make?	
Result What happened? What was the result? Be specific, and provide details, facts and figures How were things better than before?	

Star Two	Description
Situation What was the situation? What problem did you need to solve? What was the context?	
Task What was your specific task? What did you set out to achieve?	
Action What did you do? What steps did you take to solve the problem? What improvements did you make?	
Result What happened? What was the result? Be specific, and provide details, facts and figures How were things better than before?	

Star Three	Description
Situation What was the situation? What problem did you need to solve? What was the context?	
Task What was your specific task? What did you set out to achieve?	
Action What did you do? What steps did you take to solve the problem? What improvements did you make?	
Result What happened? What was the result? Be specific, and provide details, facts and figures How were things better than before?	

Star Four	Description
Situation What was the situation? What problem did you need to solve? What was the context?	
Task What was your specific task? What did you set out to achieve?	
Action What did you do? What steps did you take to solve the problem? What improvements did you make?	
Result What happened? What was the result? Be specific, and provide details, facts and figures How were things better than before?	

Star Five	Description
Situation What was the situation? What problem did you need to solve? What was the context?	
Task What was your specific task? What did you set out to achieve?	
Action What did you do? What steps did you take to solve the problem? What improvements did you make?	
Result What happened? What was the result? Be specific, and provide details, facts and figures How were things better than before?	

OVERCOMING CAREER DIFFICULTIES

'Blessed is the one who perseveres under trial because, having stood the test,
that person will receive the crown of life that the Lord has promised to those who love Him'
(James1:12).

Read the section on OVERCOMING CAREER DIFFICULTIES in the book.

Make a note of your reflections and thoughts here.

Identify your learning experiences.

You can learn a lot from overcoming difficulties, obstacles and barriers that impede your career and career progression. God does not promise us an easy journey, but He does not abandon us! We all have to overcome difficulties in our lives, or go through experiences which don't go as we'd planned or like, including working with difficult people or bosses, being made redundant, or being sacked, missing out on promotions, or not got the job you desperately wanted. You could have stayed in a job you hated because you needed the money, or because it fitted with other areas of your life, such as caring for family members, or you felt there was nothing else you could do.

Often our personal lives affect our working lives, and we don't realise the skills and qualities we've gained through persevering and overcoming these challenges. What challenges have you overcome? What were the results? What did you learn? What have you achieved in overcoming obstacles in your career life? Often these are the stories where we really learn about ourselves. Use the CARL Model of Reflection[2], to flesh out these achievements.

Briefly describe the Context of what you had to overcome. Then list the Actions you took noting specific details. Make a note of the Results and importantly what you have Learned.

ACTIVITY 20: YOUR CARL ACHIEVEMENTS

Purpose

To identify challenges overcome, battles won and what you have learned from these experiences.

Prayer
Father God, thank you for bringing me safely through the challenges and obstacles in my life.
Help me identify what I have learned from these experiences.
In Jesus name, Amen.

Instructions

1. Start by making a list of things you have overcome.

2. Then use the CARL Reflection model to flesh them out, paying close attention to what you have learned about yourself. Tell the story of what happened.

- Explain the Context.
  Write down all the details of the context you can remember. Be as specific as you can.

- State the Actions you took.
  Make a note of all the actions and steps you took in this situation. You might need to go back over them to list them in the right order.

- Note the Results or the outcome.
  Record the outcome. Explain the difference made as a result of your actions.

- Describe what have you Learned.
  List everything you have learned from this situation. What you would do differently given the chance to do it again?

CARL One	Description
Context Write down as many details as you can remember about the context.	
Action What did you do? What steps did you take to overcome the situation? What actions did you take to overcome the challenge?	
Result What was the result? How were things better than before?	
Learning What did you learn? What would you do differently in a similar situation again? What did you learn about yourself?	

CARL Two	Description
Context Write down as many details as you can remember about the context.	
Action What did you do? What steps did you take to overcome the situation? What actions did you take to overcome the challenge?	
Result What was the result? How were things better than before?	
Learning What did you learn? What would you do differently in a similar situation again? What did you learn about yourself?	

CARL Three	Description
Context Write down as many details as you can remember about the context.	
Action What did you do? What steps did you take to overcome the situation? What actions did you take to overcome the challenge?	
Result What was the result? How were things better than before?	
Learning What did you learn? What would you do differently in a similar situation again? What did you learn about yourself?	

CARL Four	Description
Context Write down as many details as you can remember about the context.	
Action What did you do? What steps did you take to overcome the situation? What actions did you take to overcome the challenge?	
Result What was the result? How were things better than before?	
Learning What did you learn? What would you do differently in a similar situation again? What did you learn about yourself?	

ACTIVITY 21:
YOUR ACHIEVEMENTS REVIEWED

Purpose

To review your satisfying achievements and career difficulties to identify the key themes and takeaways from achievements and obstacles overcome.

Prayer
Father God remind me of the satisfying achievements in my life which are relevant
to my career journey. Show me where I have had to overcome and the lessons You want
me to learn from these unique experiences.
In Jesus name, Amen.

Instructions

Reflect on your STAR and CARL Achievements to see where God was at work in each situation. Write your responses to the questions below.

* Where was God in your examples?

* Did He feel close or far away? Why do you think this?

* Did you hear His still small voice inspiring you? What was He telling you?

✿ How was He making good out of the bad?

✿ How was He working on your character through what you have learned?

✿ How did your faith impact what you did, your successes and your battles won?

✿ Are there any themes or patterns you can see? Make a note of them here.

YOUR FRUIT

'You did not choose me, but I chose you and appointed you so that you might go and bear fruit—fruit that will last—and so that whatever you ask in my name the Father will give you'
(John 15:16).

Read the section on YOUR FRUIT in the book.

Make a note of your reflections and thoughts here.

What fruit are you bearing?

The fruit you bear through your work and career is made up of three things:

1. The good works God has planned for you in advance (Ephesians 2:10).

Think about your current job and the jobs you've had. What are the outcomes? What are you providing? What are you selling? What is your product, your service? What do other people get from your work?

2. The development of your character (Galatians 5:22-23).

This is the fruit of your impact on other lives and becoming more like Jesus. How is the fruit of the Spirit displayed through the work you do?

3. Your Christian witness to others, believers and non-believers.

As a Christian you are to be recognised by your fruit. You can't bear fruit on your own! Jesus reminds us we have to be connected to Him in order to grow fruit (John 15:5).

Understanding that God is growing fruit in your career helps you to see your career from God's perspective, especially when things don't seem to be going well. Are you going through a time of trial? What fruit is God growing in you? When you are flourishing, what fruit are you displaying for others to see?

ACTIVITY 22:
IDENTIFY YOUR FRUIT

Purpose

To identify fruit God is growing in you in three areas of your life, the good works God planned for you, the development of your character and your Christian witness to others.

Prayer

Father God, thank You for the good works You have planned for me. Help me
to stay close to You as You develop the fruit of character in me.
Please build my confidence to witness to non-believers.
In Jesus name, Amen.

Instructions

1. Your Good Works – identify the fruit of your good works.

Think about your current role and answer the following questions. Your job description, if you have one, should provide clues about your good works.

- What are the contributions you make?

- What are your 'good works'?

- What are you providing, selling, doing?

2. Your Character Development – how is God growing your character?

Ask God to reveal how the fruit of the Spirit is displayed in your work, then answer the questions below.

❀   Think back over your day – how did you respond to challenging situations?

❀   Think back over your week – how is God developing your character through your work?

❀   Think back over your year – is there any fruitful change in your character you can identify?

3. Your Christian Witness – how is your Christian witness growing?

Write your answers to the questions below.

❀   How is God using you at work to witness to other people?

❀   Is there any way you feel God prompting you to reach out to non-Christians?

Reflection

✸ Can you see any connections or themes between these three types of fruit? Make a note of these.

✸ Do you feel God prompting you to make any changes? Make a note of your thoughts here.

YOUR BLESSINGS

'From the fullness of his grace we have all received one blessing after another'
(John 1:16 NIV 1984).

Read the section on YOUR BLESSINGS in the book.

Make a note of your reflections and thoughts here.

How has God blessed you?

When you flourish at work, this is God's blessing to you. This blessing entails spiritual, emotional, physical, psychological and material blessings, everything you need to live a fully blessed life.

God is at work blessing us regardless of the circumstances of our lives. Sometimes it's easier to notice those blessings when you are flourishing at work, when things are going well, when you are using your skills and talents to the full, when there are great results, and you feel 'in the flow.'

Look back over your career journey. What blessings can you spot? When were you doing work which aligned with your talents, skills and strengths? When were you flourishing, and what was the cause? When were you blessed with great colleagues? When were you able to bless other people? How did God bless you in times of adversity?

Knowing how God has blessed you sets you up for success and can change your attitude to your career. This reminds you that God has a good plan for your life, and by being blessed in your career you can be a blessing to others.

ACTIVITY 23:
YOUR CAREER BLESSINGS

Purpose

To identify your blessings by reviewing your career journey.

Prayer
Father God, thank You so much for all the blessings You have poured out on me during my career. Help me to recognise them as I look back over my career journey.
In Jesus name, Amen.

Instructions

Work quickly to list all the ways God is blessing you in your work. Include spiritual, emotional, physical, psychological and material blessings.

1. Start with times when you were flourishing. Use the questions below to identify how God blessed you.

- Did God bless you with meaningful work which made use of your talents, skills and strengths?
- Did He bless you with great colleagues?
- Was it with opportunities for growth and development?
- Was it with a time of stability, peace and prosperity?

Make a note of your blessings here.

2. Now move onto times when you were languishing. Use the questions below as a guide.

- What did you learn through this time?
- Was God growing your character?
- What was He teaching you?
- How are you benefitting now from what you went through?

Make a note of how God blessed you in this time, remember the gift of hindsight!

3. Think back over the last day, week and month and consider how God is blessing you now.

- How is God blessing you now?

4. Spend some time thanking God for all these blessings and settle them in your heart by knowing God loves to bless you.

YOUR VALUES

'Again, the kingdom of heaven is like a merchant looking for fine pearls.
When he found one of great value, he went away and sold everything he had and bought it'
(Matthew 13:45-46).

Read the section on YOUR VALUES in the book.

Make a note of your reflections and thoughts here.

Identify your own values.

Values are personal and specific. They are the things you hold in the highest regard. Your values guide your decision making, priorities and actions. There can be a huge source of tension when your values are not aligned with the prevailing values in your work setting. Things can feel wrong or out of place and this can become a source of dissatisfaction. Conversely when your values are aligned with those in your work setting, this can be a source of flourishing and deep satisfaction in your work. The things you treasure in your heart can give you clues about your values (Matthew 6:21).

Look back over your career journey, identifying the peak career experiences and times you were flourishing, when God was blessing you, as well as the low points in your career. Then consider what values were present which either made this event or time really satisfying for you, or conversely what values were missing or jarring which contributed to the low points.

Reviewing your values is not a quick activity! It takes time to reflect on what's important to you as well as the things on which you would struggle to compromise. Take your time with this activity, leave it and go back to it a few times to see what really resonates or what gives you a sense of peace

ACTIVITY 24:
KNOW YOUR VALUES

Purpose

To identify and understand your values.

Prayer
Father God, I ask Your Holy Spirit to reveal the values which are most important to me.
In Jesus name, Amen.

Split cue / 2 lines!

Instructions

Choose one of these methods.

Whichever method you choose limit yourself to no more than six top values.

They need to be meaningful for you and you should be able to remember them!

Method One

1. Review your career journey, noting the times when you were flourishing.

   * Which values were present which helped you to flourish?

2. Next consider your low points.

   * Which values were missing or jarring contributing to these low points?   *sounds odd.*

3. Identify any themes or consistencies and underline the ones which feel particularly true to your sense of self.

Method Two

1. Grab a stack of yellow stickies, set a timer for 10 minutes and write a different value on each stickie, without judging what you're writing. To do this activity interactively you could identify your values with a friend or family member to keep the ideas flowing and the energy high.

Use the question

- "What's important to you?" Keep going until your timer alarm sounds.

2. Then group your stickies into categories which feature similar ideas.

3. Think of one word which encapsulates the ideas for each group.

4. Describe what this word means to you in one sentence.

5. Write your values here.

Value Word	Description - A sentence to explain what this value means to you

Rate these value words.

♣ Which ones are really important to you? Make a note of them here.

7. Whichever method you use, a day or two later, revisit your value words. Note down an example of when this value is present or is not present in your work at the moment, which could indicate a need for a change.

♣ Then ask yourself how do I display this value?

For each one think of an example of when it is apparent in your career. Write your reflections here.

REFLECTION ACTIVITY:
YOUR CAREER EXPERIENCE SHIELD

Purpose

To draw your own career experience shield as a summary of what you have learned about yourself and your career to date.

Prayer

Father God thank You so much for all the career experiences You have given me,
for my achievements, and things I have overcome, for the Godly fruit I display,
and Your blessings. Thank You for the values You have given me, help me identify
the ones which are most important to You.
In Jesus name, Amen.

Instructions

Review your career experiences and use the template to create your career experience shield. Use brief words and pictures as items on your shield, so that it encapsulates all the important elements of your career experience.

Consider these questions.

- ❈ What are the key themes gained from your career journey?

- ❈ What are the lessons learned?

✻   What are your key achievements?

✻   What Godly 'fruit' are you displaying?

✻   How could you display more Godly 'fruit' in your career?

✻   What blessings God has given you in your career?

🕷 What was your experience of God's grace when you were flourishing in your career?

🕷 How did you experience blessings when you were not flourishing?

🕷 What are your top values?

Use the shield outline on the next page and use your answers to write words or draw pictures on your shield which represent your career experiences. I recommend you really get your creative juices flowing and use colour and drawings as far as possible.

YOUR CAREER EXPERIENCE SHIELD

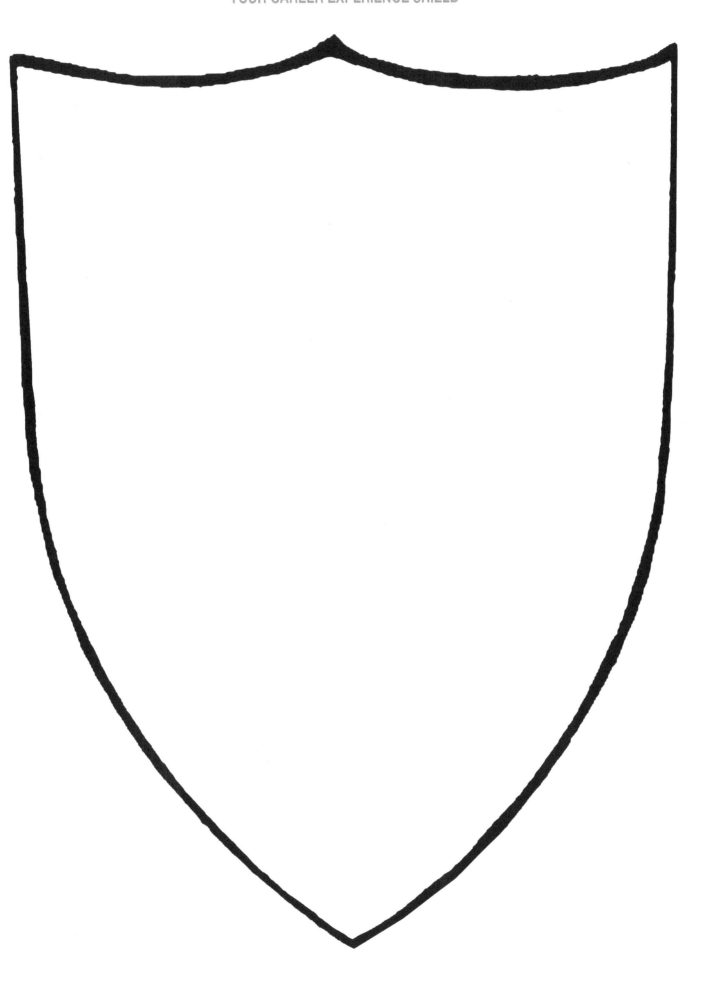

6

God's Grace For You

Gifts
Relationships
Abilities
Curiosities
Experiences

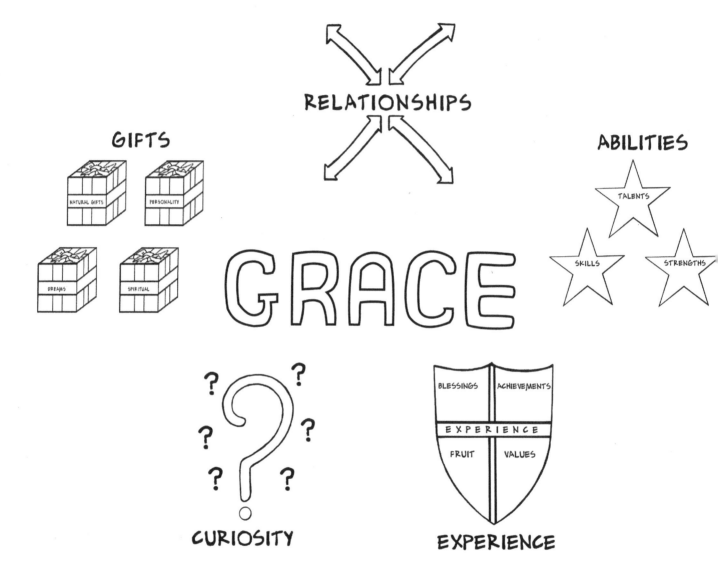

MODULE 6 - GOD'S GRACE FOR YOU

'For it is by grace you have been saved, through faith – and this is not from yourselves,
it is the gift of God – not by works, so that no one can boast'
(Ephesians 2:8-9).

God has given you all the GRACE you need for your career and as you have used this learning guide to help you explore your Gifts, Relationships, Abilities, Curiosities and Experiences you will have seen the uniqueness in the way you are 'knit together' (Psalm 139:13) and how your story is unique. God's grace makes a difference in your career and can impact the choices you make for your future.

Jesus says to His followers, "You are the salt of the earth" (Matthew 5:13) and as Christians we are meant to bring a distinctive flavour to our work situations, similar to the way salt flavours food. We do this is by embracing the values of God's Kingdom in our workplaces. These are Kingdom values that people who are members of God's Kingdom display, often counter-cultural and when we demonstrate them in our working lives, they bring honour to God, and help us grow more like Jesus. They demonstrate God's grace in our lives and the distinctiveness being a follower of Jesus can make to your working life.

You could have completed a career exploration without any mention of Christian faith, but it is my view that God's perspective makes all the difference. When you understand He has made you uniquely for a purpose and you find the career path He prepared for you; you will find you can flourish at work.

In this module you will explore which Kingdom Values God has placed on your heart and how you might express them in your career. You will also review all the GRACE Unwrapped God has given you for your career and display it in one place. Finally, you will have the opportunity to draw up the Career Blueprint God has for your future using all the clues He has left along the way. Your Career Blueprint lays the foundation for God's purposes for your career and from it you will compose your Career Purpose.

Prayer

Father God, as I explore Your Kingdom values, and draw together all the strands of your GRACE for my career, prompt me through Your Holy Spirit to construct a career blueprint which is authentic and exciting and points to Your purpose for my career.

In Jesus name, Amen.

Write your own prayer here.

KINGDOM VALUES

'Those who live according to the sinful nature have their minds set on what that nature desires; but those who live in accordance with the Spirit have their minds set on what the Spirit desires'
(Romans 8:5)

Read the section on KINGDOM VALUES in the book.

Make a note of your reflections and thoughts here.

Identifying Your Kingdom Values.

God's Kingdom values remind us of the spiritual element of our working lives and the difference following Jesus makes in our careers, but they are not always easy to adopt and display.

Kingdom values are driven by love for God and love for others. They are often counter-cultural, just as Jesus was counter-cultural. Displaying Kingdom values in the workplace can be challenging, but we have not been left to do this on our own. The Holy Spirit leads and guides us in all things, as we make a decision, a choice, to co-operate with Him and display Kingdom values in our careers.

As you discern the Kingdom values God wants you to focus on, it's important you use your own words and make sure you know what the Kingdom value means to you, as well as how it's evident in your work or career. As you ponder and pray about the Kingdom values God wants you to display in your career, make a note of them, and find a Bible verse or two to pin this value to God's Kingdom. Then describe what this Kingdom value means to you in practice.

You could argue all these Kingdom values are important, and I would agree! However, there is a time and season for everything (Ecclesiastes 3:1) and therefore I recommend you focus on the two or three which really tug at your heart strings.

ACTIVITY 25:
IDENTIFY YOUR KINGDOM VALUES

Purpose

To identify Kingdom values God wants you to display in your career and workplace.

Prayer
Father God, thank You for the wonderful example set by Jesus in displaying Kingdom values.
Help me to grow more and more like Jesus as I display Kingdom values in my career.
In Jesus name, Amen.

Instructions

1. Spend some time in prayer and worship.

2. Consider which two or three Kingdom values resonate with you and your career.

3. Make a note of these and describe what they mean in your own words.

4. Find a verse or two in the Bible to pin this value to God's Kingdom. You will find a selection to get you started in Appendix Three.

5. Rate yourself on a scale of 1 - 10 where 10 indicates you display this value all the time, and 1 indicates you do not.

Kingdom Value	Description - A sentence describing this value in your own words
Bible Verses	
How well am I demonstrating this value in my career?	
	1 2 3 4 5 6 7 8 9 10

Kingdom Value	Description - A sentence describing this value in your own words

Bible Verses

How well am I demonstrating this value in my career?

1   2   3   4   5   6   7   8   9   10

Kingdom Value	Description - A sentence describing this value in your own words

Bible Verses

How well am I demonstrating this value in my career?

1   2   3   4   5   6   7   8   9   10

6. Reflect on your Kingdom values using the questions below as a guide.

     ✸   Consider what are the overlaps with your personal values?

     ✸   What are the contradictions or the clashes?

     ✸   How might this Kingdom value become more prevalent in your career?

     ✸   What steps can you take to make this happen?

You could share your thoughts with one of your Trusted Friends. Remember we are all works in progress! Aligning yourself with God's Kingdom values and becoming more like Jesus is an ongoing process.

YOUR GRACE UNWRAPPED

'And God will generously provide all you need. Then you will always have everything
you need and plenty left over to share with others'
(2 Corinthians 9:8 NLT).

Read the section on YOUR GRACE UNWRAPPED in the book.

Make a note of your reflections and thoughts here.

Unwrap God's GRACE for your career.

God has given you everything you need for your career; the skills, the dreams, the experiences, your personality. When you figure out what all these things are, the way God put you together, you can identify the blueprint which makes you unique and then be more able to align your work with God's purpose in mind. When they are gathered together and displayed in one place where you can see them, you can then make decisions about what you want to do with them.

Questions to consider include: Which skills does God want you to use more of? How have your experiences shaped you for what God wants you to do next? Which things are you going to use straight away? Which areas need time to grow and develop a bit? Which ideas need a bit more exploration for the future in terms of how you might use them? What have you learnt about the unique package of GRACE God has given you for your career?

Think of the image of unwrapping Christmas presents, as you gather together all the ideas and themes you have uncovered from the GRACE God has given you for your career and collect them all into one place.

ACTIVITY 26:
YOUR GRACE DISPLAYED

Purpose

To display all the GRACE God has given you for your career in one place.

Prayer

Father God, thank You for the amazing unique GRACE You have given me for my career.
Guide me with Your Holy Spirit as I consolidate all You have provided for my career
in my personal GRACE filled package.
In Jesus name, Amen.

Instructions

This might take some time, so make a cuppa and settle down somewhere uninterrupted. You could put some background worship music on. This is your time with God to unwrap His GRACE for your career.

Your aim is to summarise your findings, to begin the process of condensing them into one space.

1. Review the Reflection Activities at the end of each chapter. Use the following questions as a guide.

2. Fill each GRACE box with words, or images of the main findings from each area of your exploration.

Remember this is a summary, so condense your thoughts and ideas – be precise!

Your Gifts

- ❋ Of all the Gifts you identified which ones really stand out for you?
- ❋ Is it your natural gifts, or something about your personality, or one of your dreams or is God prompting you to use your spiritual gifts?

Write down a few words or short phrases which crystallise your thoughts in the Gifts box

Your Relationships

- ❋ What have you learned about your relationship with God?
- ❋ Is He prompting you to spend more time with Him in prayer, in worship, or reading the Bible?
- ❋ What is He saying to you about your career?
- ❋ Who are your Trusted Friends and how might you nurture your relationships with these people?
- ❋ Who is in your Wider Network?
- ❋ How do you connect with them?
- ❋ Who are your Role Models?
- ❋ Which one is the most significant for you and why?

✸ What one lesson can you learn from them to apply in your life?

Make a note of your main thoughts in the Relationships box.

Your Abilities

✸ What did you discover about your talents, skills and strengths?

✸ Which ones resonate with you the most?

✸ Which ones do you think God is asking you to use more?

✸ Which skills would you like to develop?

✸ Which unrealised strengths would you like to grow so that you feel more energised and engaged in your career?

Note down key themes, using different coloured pens if this helps in the Abilities box.

Your Curiosities

✸ What stood out for you as you explored your Vine of Curiosity?

✸ Are there topics in your education which are important, or is there knowledge you have gained which you would like to put to good use?

✸ How about the subjects which interest you; which ones would you like to pick up now and pursue?

✸ What things moved your heart to compassion and action?

✸ Do you sense God's prompting for you to do more in this area?

✸ What do you know in your inner wisdom? How do you feel about this? Is it time to act on this?

✸ What if anything, has God revealed to you?

Record anything which really stands out for you, that you want to take forward in the Curiosities box.

Your Experiences

✸ What are the themes which stand out for you from your career journey?

✸ What have you gained from your achievements and the difficulties you have overcome?

✸ What fruit have you seen?

✸ How has God blessed you?

✸ What are your key values, the things most important to you?

✸ How do they relate to God's Kingdom values?

✸ Are there any of these which particularly resonate for you as important for the next stage in your career?

Highlight things which are really important to you and make a note of them in the Experiences box.

At the end why not draw a colourful outline for each box to remind yourself this GRACE is gift-wrapped by God, intended for good for your future.

YOUR GRACE UNWRAPPED

GIFTS		RELATIONSHIPS

ABILITIES

CURIOSTIES		EXPERIENCES
GIFTS		

YOUR CAREER BLUEPRINT

'Remember, there is only one foundation, the one already laid: Jesus Christ'
(1 Corinthians 3:11 MSG).

Read the section on YOUR CAREER BLUEPRINT in the book.

Make a note of your reflections and thoughts here.

Outline your own career blueprint.

God has the blueprint for your career drawn up, and you will have discovered all the elements of it through the activities in this book. Your career blueprint provides the framework for your career from God's perspective, the way He created you to do the work He planned for you.

The blueprint allows you to see all the pieces needed to plan for your career, from your personality, to what your key skills are, your interests, your values and your experiences. To draw up your own blueprint you need to revisit your GRACE displayed and ask some questions. What themes stand out? Which things seem to come up time and time again? What patterns or career clues can you identify? What things are unique about you? Which items cause your heart to beat a bit more? How do your themes relate to God's Kingdom values? Which elements make you smile with delight and say 'Yes, that's me!'

ACTIVITY 27:
YOUR CAREER BLUEPRINT

Purpose

To identify the unique career blueprint God has planned for you.

Prayer

Father God, thank You for the career blueprint You designed for me. Lead me by Your Holy Spirit to see the important themes and how they link together as I draw up my blueprint.
In Jesus name, Amen.

Instructions

1. Look at each area of your GRACE Displayed and highlight things which excite you or things which seem significant.

2. Write a sentence or two answering each of the following questions based on things highlighted in your GRACE Displayed. Use the following questions as a guide.

Who are you?

- Which things from your GRACE Displayed really connect with who God made you to be, the person He created in your mother's womb? This could include your personality, your natural gifts and talents, your values.

- From all the information you have gathered what makes you unique?

- Write a sentence or two describing who you are based on the GRACE you have unwrapped.

What are you good at?

✤   Make a note of your talents, skills and strengths, and how you use them in a combination which is unique to you.

✤   Think about your achievements, what have you discovered you are good at from the challenges you have overcome, or successes achieved?

✤   Briefly note things down which seem particularly relevant or impactful to you from your answers to the questions above.

What has God already done in your career?

✤   Which dreams have been realised, prayers answered, blessings received?

✤   Which significant people has God connected you with for the next stage of your career?

✤   Which paths He has directed you down?

✸   What specific occasions or times in your past career do you feel God might be using to prepare you for the future?

✸   What fruit have you seen in your career?

✸   How has God blessed you?

✸   How did your education or knowledge or interests set you up for your career so far?

✸   Review your thoughts and make a note of anything significant here.

What career clues has God given you?

* What significant dreams has God given you, in your childhood or more recently, which are as yet unrealised?

* Which compassions make your heart beat a bit faster so that you feel you need to act on them?

* Which interests intrigue you the most?

* What fruit do you think God might want you to grow or develop?

* Is there a spiritual gift you feel drawn to explore?

* What does your inner wisdom tell you?

❀ Has God given you any specific revelations?

❀ Which Kingdom value does God want you to develop in your career?

❀ Write a summary paragraph outlining the career clues God has given you.

Remember, you are unique just as God made you so as you review what you have written ask yourself,

❀ Is this me?

❀ Is this authentic?

You should feel a sense of excitement or a sense of peace about how your blueprint uniquely fits you.

Take some time to thank God for this.

YOUR CAREER PURPOSE

'Many are the plans in a person's heart,
but it is the Lord's purpose that prevails'
(Proverbs 19:21).

Read the section on YOUR CAREER PURPOSE in the book.

Make a note of your reflections and thoughts here.

Write your own career purpose.

The great thing about your career blueprint is that it points to God's overall purpose for your career. So, when you've drawn up your blueprint, ask yourself, 'What does this tell me about God's purpose for my career?'

Come up with a sentence or two. This career purpose is the bedrock for decisions and choices you make about your future career.

Review you career blueprint and ask God, "What does all this tell me about Your purpose for my career?" Write down anything which comes to mind. The words you write should you make you shout a resounding "YES!"

ACTIVITY 28:
YOUR CAREER PURPOSE

Purpose

To identify your own personal career purpose.

Prayer
Father God, thank You that I am uniquely designed
and help me identify my career purpose.
In Jesus name, Amen.

Instructions

1. Prayerfully invite the Holy Spirit to inspire you.

2. Review your career blueprint and ask yourself ...

   ✿   What does this tell me about God's purpose for my career?

3. Write down the words which come to mind, let this flow as a stream of consciousness.

4. Turn this into a sentence or two which describes your career purpose.

5. Notice how you feel about this.

   ✿   Are you excited?

   ✿   Do you have a sense of deep inner peace?

   ✿   Are you clear that this is God's purpose for you?

6. Let this settle for a day or two before returning to confirm it or make any changes you think God might be prompting you to add.

7. When you sense it's right for you put it somewhere you can see it, or memorise it, so that you have it hand when you need it.

REFLECTION ACTIVITY: YOUR CAREER IN GOD'S HANDS

'But to each one of us grace has been given as Christ apportioned it'
(Ephesians 4:7).

Purpose

This final module has focussed on career exploration from God's perspective. You've considered His Kingdom values and how they relate to your career. You've unwrapped the GRACE God has given you and displayed it somewhere prominent. From this you've identified important themes and drawn up your own career blueprint and then you've penned your own career purpose.

Prayer

Father God, thank You for everything You have given me, and everything You have done in my career. Guide me as I take all I have learned about myself and use it to take the next steps in my career journey.
In Jesus name, Amen.

Instructions

1. Take time to thank God. Write your own prayer on the opposite page.

2. Thank Him for His Kingdom values, and how He inspires you through His Holy Spirit.

3. Thank Him for all the GRACE you have unwrapped for your career. Thank Him for how He has been and is at work in your career using all things for good.

4. Thank Him for your career blueprint which makes sense of all the GRACE He has given you.

5. And thank Him for your career purpose and ask Him to open doors for your work to be aligned with this.

6. Take time to thank God for leading you and holding you and your career in His loving hands, as it says in Psalm 139.10 'even there your hand will guide me, your right hand will hold me fast.'

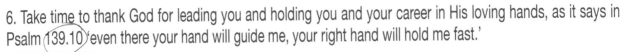

WRITE YOUR OWN PRAYER OF THANKS

APPENDIX ONE: SPIRITUAL GIFTS SELF-ASSESSMENT CHECKLIST

Purpose

To review your spiritual gifts and how you use them in your career or at work.

Introduction

Sometimes it's not obvious what your spiritual gifts are so this checklist has been designed to help you explore what you think your spiritual gifts might be. This checklist will give you an idea of what they are, but you won't really know unless you test them out! Spiritual gifts are used in the service of Christ to build up the Kingdom of God so as you complete this checklist think back on your own experience in serving Christ, in both your work and personal life.

Instructions

Pray for discernment from God as you review this checklist.

Prayer

Father God, You have given us spiritual gifts
to help build up the body of Christ,
reveal to me the gifts You have given me
as I work through this checklist.

(In Jesus name, Amen.

Write your own prayer here.

2. Choose a wise and discerning Christian to go through it with you if possible.

3. For each spiritual gift think back on your own experience of serving Christ and consider if you think you have the gift. Your choices are 'yes', 'maybe' or 'no.'

4. Consider how you might be using this gift in your current workplace.

5. Complete the reflections at the end of the checklist.

The following tables are adapted from: Definitions Revd. Lee Proudlove; *Your SHAPE for God's Service*, by Amiel Mary E. Osmaston[1]; *S.H.A.P.E.* by Erik Rees.[2]

ADMINISTRATION			
A gift given to certain members of the body of Christ to enable others to work effectively together for the benefit of Christ's Kingdom.			
Luke 14:28-30; Acts 6:1-7; 1 Corinthians 12:28; Exodus 18:13-26			
If you have the gift of administration you are likely good at developing strategies, planning and goal setting. You might find you get involved in projects to make them more efficient and effective, or you could be managing or coordinating several different activities, and you thrive on organising people, tasks and events. You easily visualise what needs to be done.	Yes	Maybe	No
If Yes, how are you using this spiritual gift in your work to build up the body of Christ?			

APOSTLESHIP			
A gift given to certain members of the body of Christ to lay true foundations for a new work of God. (The original Greek meaning of the word is "sent one" – sent with authority or as an ambassador).			
Acts 15:22-35; 1 Corinthians 12:28; 2 Corinthians 12:12; Galatians 2:7-10; Ephesians 4:11-14; Romans 1:5; Acts 13:2-3			
If you have the gift of apostleship you may find you are drawn to opportunities to pioneer new things and have a keen sense of vision for the mission of God's Kingdom. You find you adapt easily to new situations and love to be an Ambassador for Christ. You may enjoy finding ways to share your faith in different cultures and environments and are keen to try new things for Christ.	Yes	Maybe	No
If Yes, how are you using this spiritual gift in your work to build up the body of Christ?			

CRAFTSMANSHIP			
A gift given to certain members of the body of Christ to plan, build, and work with their hands in construction environments to accomplish multiple ministry applications.			
Exodus 31:3-11; 35:31-35; Acts 9:36-39			
If you have the gift of craftsmanship you may find you are drawn to opportunities to work in a practical and artistic way with wood, materials, paints, metals or glass to create things that are useful or beautiful for the glory of God. You may find yourself mending things or designing things that will be of benefit to the Kingdom of God that will draw people closer to Him in worship, and you enjoy serving God creatively with your hands.	Yes	Maybe	No
If Yes, how are you using this spiritual gift in your work to build up the body of Christ?			

CREATIVE COMMUNICATION			
A gift given to certain members of the body of Christ to communicate creatively to share God's Word to believers and non-believers alike.			
Psalm 150; 2 Samuel 6:14-15; Mark 4:1-2, 33			
If you have the gift of creative communication, you may find you are drawn to opportunities to use the arts to communicate God's love and truth. This could be through music, drama, dance, writing, poetry, photography, graphics, art and you will love exploring how your artistry can help build up God's Kingdom through creative activities that glorify God and enrich worship.	Yes	Maybe	No
If Yes, how are you using this spiritual gift in your work to build up the body of Christ?			

DISCERNMENT			
A gift given to certain members of the body of Christ to discern the spiritual reality behind a certain situation or persons behaviour.			
Matthew 16:21-23; Acts 16:16-18; 1 Corinthians 12:10; 1 John 4:1-6			
If you have the gift of discernment, it's likely that you find you can tune into the spiritual environment to know when forces opposing God are active. You may also find you are given insight into the reasons for what seems to be happening, and that you can determine truth from falsehood. You will have clarity about whether something is from God or not and be able to test the spirits and look for fruit of the Holy Spirit.	Yes	Maybe	No
If Yes, how are you using this spiritual gift in your work to build up the body of Christ?			

ENCOURAGEMENT			
A gift given to certain members of the body of Christ to minister encouragement so other members of the body are strengthened and equipped.			
Romans 12:8; Hebrews 10:24-25; Acts 11:22-24; Acts15:30-32			
If you have the gift of encouragement you probably find you draw alongside people regularly to encourage them in life, and their walk with Jesus. You love to strengthen and reassure people who are discouraged, and to help them put their trust and hope in God. You often see the best in people and point out their gifts and strengths and how that impacts the body of Christ.	Yes	Maybe	No
If Yes, how are you using this spiritual gift in your work to build up the body of Christ?			

EVANGELISM			
A gift given to certain members of the body of Christ to effectively communicate the message of the gospel as a witness for Jesus Christ and to bring people into God's Kingdom.			
Acts 8:5-6; Acts 8:26-40; Acts 14:21; Luke 19:1-10			
If you have the gift of evangelism you may find you get excited about sharing your faith with non-believers and you seek opportunities to talk to people about spiritual matters. You have a sense when non-believers are receptive to Christ and long to bring more people into the Kingdom. You find you are drawn to evangelistic opportunities and have a heart for God's lost sheep.	Yes	Maybe	No
If Yes, how are you using this spiritual gift in your work to build up the body of Christ?			

FAITH			
A gift given to certain members of the body of Christ to discern with confidence the will and purposes of God for the future of His work.			
Acts 11:22-24; Romans 4:18-21; 1 Corinthians 12:9; 1 Corinthians13:2; Hebrews 11:1			
If you have the gift of faith you believe firmly in God and inspire others to trust Him. You may find yourself praying with passion and perseverance and expect God to answer your prayers, knowing that He will overcome all issues. You may be willing to take risks for your faith putting complete confidence in Jesus. You will be keen to step out in faith to see what God will do.	Yes	Maybe	No
If Yes, how are you using this spiritual gift in your work to build up the body of Christ?			

GIVING			
A gift given to certain members of the body of Christ to contribute their material resources to Christ's work with liberality and cheerfulness.			
Mark 12:41-44; Romans 12:8; 2 Corinthians 8:1-7; Luke 21:1-4			
If you have the gift of giving, you will find yourself giving time or money most cheerfully. You will be contributing and supporting Christian ventures that support and enable God's Kingdom to grow. You will be managing your finances and resources so that you can give away whatever God asks of you and you will long to support those less fortunate than yourself. You may also have a special ability to make money that can be used for God's purposes.	Yes	Maybe	No
If Yes, how are you using this spiritual gift in your work to build up the body of Christ?			

HEALING			
A gift given to certain members of the body of Christ to pray with confidence for the healing of others.			
Acts 3:1-10; Acts 9:32-41; Acts 28:7-10; 1 Corinthians 12:9, 28, 30; Mark 2:1-12			
If you have the gift of healing you may find you consistently pray for people and they are healed. You may be drawn to people who are suffering physically, mentally, emotionally or spiritually and know that God can heal them supernaturally. You may also find you care deeply for these people and long to see God heal them. You may also be able to bring comfort, relief and restoration to people who are suffering.	Yes	Maybe	No
If Yes, how are you using this spiritual gift in your work to build up the body of Christ?			

HELPS			
A gift given to certain members of the body of Christ to invest the talents they have in the life and ministry of others to help them achieve their God-given potential			
Mark 15:40-41; Acts 9:36; Romans 16:1-2; 1 Corinthians 12:28			
If you have the gift of helps you may find you are drawn to people who are in need and long to help them. You may be able to spot needs easily and seek to help them from your own resources. You are drawn to people in difficult circumstances and feel a deep compassion for them and long to see them move into their God-given potential.	Yes	Maybe	No
If Yes, how are you using this spiritual gift in your work to build up the body of Christ?			

HOSPITALITY			
A gift given to certain members of the body of Christ to offer an open house and a warm welcome for the benefit of others.			
Acts 16:14-15; Romans 12:13; Romans 16:23; Hebrews 13:1-2; 1 Peter 4:9			
If you have the gift of hospitality, you find it easy to welcome people and help them to feel at ease. You like to make people feel valued and cared for by meeting their needs for food, warmth, comfort and shelter. You are likely to really enjoy fellowship and seek out opportunities to provide comfortable spaces for this. You look out for people who are new and welcome them, and you draw in people who are shy or lonely so that they can feel a sense of belong to the body of Christ.	Yes	Maybe	No
If Yes, how are you using this spiritual gift in your work to build up the body of Christ?			

INTERCESSION			
A gift given to certain members of the body of Christ to stand in the gap in prayer for someone, something, or someplace, believing for profound results.			
Hebrews 7:25; Colossians 1:9-12, Colossians 4:12; James 5:14-16; Romans 8:26-27; John 17:9-26			
If you have the gift of intercession you will find yourself praying in all and any circumstances. You will make time to pray for other people and situations expecting God to hear your prayers and answer them. You may be very aware of the spiritual battle and see prayer as a weapon of love. You may respond to the Holy Spirit's prompting to pray and try to stay in God's will for a person, or situation.	Yes	Maybe	No
If Yes, how are you using this spiritual gift in your work to build up the body of Christ?			

INTERPRETATION OF TONGUES			
A gift given to certain members of the body of Christ to interpret a prayer or message spoken in Tongues.			
Acts 2:4-11; 1 Corinthians 12:10; 1 Corinthians 14:1-13; 1 Corinthians 14:26-28			
If you have the gift of interpretation of tongues you are willing to take the risk of sharing what you think God is saying through another person praying in tongues. You may be enabled to understand a language you have never learned and use this to build up people's faith. You may have clarity about what God is saying about a specific person or situation in a way that edifies, comforts and exhorts believers and glorifies God.	Yes	Maybe	No
If Yes, how are you using this spiritual gift in your work to build up the body of Christ?			

KNOWLEDGE			
A gift given to certain members of the body of Christ to gain spiritual understanding of a particular situation or circumstance.			
1 Corinthians 12:8; Colossians 2:2-5; Mark 2:8; John 1:45-50; John 4:16-19			
If you have the gift of knowledge, it's likely that you have insights or hunches about people and situations. You might be given specific knowledge or information from God that you could not have known naturally. You enjoy sharing your knowledge of the Bible and the Christian faith to enhance peoples' understanding of spiritual matters.	Yes	Maybe	No
If Yes, how are you using this spiritual gift in your work to build up the body of Christ?			

LEADERSHIP			
A gift given to certain members of the body of Christ to lead the church in its mission and ministry for the glory of God.			
Romans 12:8; Hebrews 13:17; Luke 22:25-26			
If you have the gift of leadership, you are likely to be drawn to leadership positions and enjoy inspiring people to follow you. You are able to share your vision of God's Kingdom with others and motivate and enable others to meet this vision in a way that you would not naturally envision, as if they are drawn by the Holy Spirit working through you. You may also be able to delegate to other people, providing opportunities for the vision to be accomplished for God's glory.	Yes	Maybe	No
If Yes, how are you using this spiritual gift in your work to build up the body of Christ?			

MERCY			
A gift given to certain members of the body of Christ to feel compassion for others and to translate that into cheerfully done deeds that reflect Christ's love.			
Matthew 9:35-36; Mark 9:41; Romans 12:8; Matthew 5:7; Mark 10:46-52; Luke 10:25-37			
If you have the gift of mercy you may find you notice other people's pain, grief and suffering and long to do something about it. You long to show people God's love and forgiveness through your own words and actions and will devote time to praying for and with people. You may find you are drawn to working in difficult circumstances, or in places where people are in need. You may also focus your time on issues of social justice and work to help restore dignity and wholeness to the glory of God.	Yes	Maybe	No
If Yes, how are you using this spiritual gift in your work to build up the body of Christ?			

MIRACLES			
A gift given to certain members of the body of Christ to pray with confidence for God to perform mighty acts establishing His Kingdom.			
Acts 9:36-42; Acts 19:11-12; Acts 20:7-12; 1 Corinthians 12:10, 28-29; John 2:1-11			
If you have the gift of miracles, you may be inspired by the Holy Spirit to pray for supernatural solutions to impossible situations and love to see God move in this way. You love how your faith and other's faith expands in response to miracles and love to see God display his power, so that people respond in awe and wonder.	Yes	Maybe	No
If Yes, how are you using this spiritual gift in your work to build up the body of Christ?			

PASTOR/SHEPHERD			
A gift given to certain members of the body of Christ to care for the emotional, physical and spiritual wellbeing of others.			
John 10:1-18; Ephesians 4:11-13; 1 Peter 5:1-4			
If you have the gift of pastoring or shepherding, you may find yourself being concerned for the full wellbeing of people and spend your time providing guidance and helping them grow in faith. You thrive in building loving relationships and find that people confide in you and turn to you for support. You will have a deep sense of responsibility for the people God has put in your care and seek to know them personally and individually making them feel special and loved.	Yes	Maybe	No
If Yes, how are you using this spiritual gift in your work to build up the body of Christ?			

PROPHECY			
A gift given to certain members of the body of Christ to com-municate God's truth calling people to a right relationship with God and/or to speak God's word in current/future situations.			
1 Corinthians 12:10, 28; 1 Corinthians 13:2; 1 Corinthians 14:1-4; Romans 12:6; 2 Peter 1:19-21			
If you have the gift of prophecy, it's probable that you will feel a compulsion to tell people a message from God. You may find that God gives you words and messages for specific people or situations, which may expose sin, lead people to repentance and forgiveness or reveal God's character and heart. You may see truths before other people and feel called to challenge them to respond. You may feel a 'certainty' about God's plan for a specific situation or person.	Yes	Maybe	No
If Yes, how are you using this spiritual gift in your work to build up the body of Christ?			

SERVICE			
A gift given to certain members of the body of Christ to discern opportunities for service to Christ and a willingness to minister in whatever way is needed.			
Acts 6:1-7; Romans 12:7; Galatians 6:10; Titus 3:14			
If you have the gift of service it's likely you will find yourself helping behind the scenes in a practical way, and that your worship of God is expressed through service to other people in the body of Christ. You may be good at spotting what needs to be done practically and find you are drawn to situations where you can be active in your support and that this is a loving service.	Yes	Maybe	No
If Yes, how are you using this spiritual gift in your work to build up the body of Christ?			

TEACHING			
A gift given to certain members of the body of Christ to communicate Biblical truth in such a way that others grow in their knowledge of Christ.			
Acts 18:24-28; Acts 20:20-21; 1 Corinthians 12:28-29; Ephesians 4:11-13; Romans 12:7			
If you have the gift of teaching you likely love to share with other people what you are learning from God's Word. You may have a knack for explaining your insights in a way that is meaningful for other people and helps them grow in their knowledge of the Bible. You are able to communicate effectively, asking thoughtful questions and encouraging people to think and grow in confidence in their faith.	Yes	Maybe	No
If Yes, how are you using this spiritual gift in your work to build up the body of Christ?			

TONGUES (SPEAKING IN TONGUES)			
A gift given to certain members of the body of Christ to pray and praise God in an unknown language or to communicate a message from God in the same way.			
Acts 2:1-13; 1 Corinthians 12:10, 28-30; 1 Corinthians 13:1; 1 Corinthians 14:1-18			
If you have the gift of speaking in tongues, you are enabled to pray in a spiritual language you have never learned. You find you use this language to worship God privately when human words are not enough to help you draw closer to God. You may feel prompted by the Holy Spirit to pray in tongues for other people to comfort and exhort them. If you pray in tongues in public worship, it's likely that there will be someone who can interpret tongues to translate.	Yes	Maybe	No
If Yes, how are you using this spiritual gift in your work to build up the body of Christ?			

WISDOM (WORDS OF WISDOM)			
A gift given to certain members of the body of Christ to know the mind of the Holy Spirit and speak wisdom into a given situation.			
Acts 6:3,10; 1 Corinthians 2:6-16; 2 Corinthians 12:8; James 3:17; Ephesians 1:8			
If you have the gift of words of wisdom you may find God inspires you with his wisdom for certain situations to build up the body of Christ. You may find that the Holy Spirit shows you God's will for a particular situation or person. You may find that people seek you out for advice and guidance based on your understanding of God's Word and your spiritual listening ears.	Yes	Maybe	No
If Yes, how are you using this spiritual gift in your work to build up the body of Christ?			

Make a note of your main Spiritual Gifts

My Main Spiritual Gifts	How I Use This Gift at Work

Read the Bible passages given in the sections above which relate to each of your four main gifts. Ask God to speak to you through these, and spend some time listening to Him.

If you're not sure if God seems to be using these gifts through you in your work, then I encourage you to pray through them with a mature Christian who can help you discern how God is using you.

APPENDIX TWO: STRENGTH DEFINITIONS FROM CAPPFINITY:STRENGTHS PROFILE

Action Motivating
You feel compelled to act immediately and decisively, being keen to learn as you go.

Adaptable Thinking
You juggle things to meet changing demands and find the best fit for your needs.

Adherence Thinking
You love to follow processes, operating firmly within rules and guidelines.

Adventure Motivating
You love to take risks and stretch yourself outside your comfort zone.

Authenticity Being
You are always true to yourself, even in the face of pressure from others.

Bounceback Motivating
You use setbacks as springboards to go on and achieve even more.

Catalyst Motivating
You love to motivate and inspire others to make things happen.

Centred Being
You have an inner composure and self-assurance, whatever the situation.

Change Agent Motivating
You are constantly involved with change, advocating for change and making it happen.

Compassion Relating
You really care about others, doing all you can to help and sympathise.

Competitive Motivating
You are constantly competing to win, wanting to perform better and be the best.

Connector Relating
You make connections between people, instinctively making links and introductions.

Counterpoint Communicating
You always bring a different viewpoint to others, whatever the situation or context.

Courage Being
You overcome your fears and do what you want to do in spite of them.

Creativity Thinking
You strive to produce work that is original, by creating and combining things in imaginative ways.

Curiosity Being
You are interested in everything, constantly seeking out new information and learning more.

Detail Thinking
You naturally focus on the small things that others easily miss, ensuring accuracy.

Drive Motivating
You are very self-motivated, pushing yourself hard to achieve what you want out of life.

Emotional Awareness Relating
You are acutely aware of the emotions and feelings of others.

Empathic Relating
You feel connected to others through your ability to understand what they are feeling.

Enabler Relating
You create the conditions for people to grow and develop for themselves.

Equality Relating
You ensure that everyone is treated equally, paying close attention to issues of fairness.

Esteem Builder Relating
You help others to believe in themselves and see what they are capable of achieving.

Explainer Communicating
You are able to simplify things so that others can understand.

Feedback Communicating
You provide fair and accurate feedback to others, to help them develop.

Gratitude Being
You are constantly thankful for the positive things in your life.

Growth Motivating
You are always looking for ways to grow and develop, whatever you are doing.

Humility Being
You are happy to stay in the background, giving others credit for your contributions.

Humour Communicating
You see the funny side of almost everything that happens - and make a joke of it.

Improver Motivating
You constantly look for better ways of doing things and how things can be improved.

APPENDIX THREE: BIBLE VERSES FOR KINGDOM VALUES

Here are a selection of verses you can use to pin to your Kingdom values.

Excellence

- 'But you are a chosen people, a royal priesthood, a holy nation, God's special possession, that you may declare the praises of Him who called you out of darkness into His wonderful light' (1 Peter 2:9).

- 'Then this Daniel became distinguished above all the other high officials and satraps, because an excellent spirit was in him. And the king planned to set him over the whole kingdom' (Daniel 6:3 ESV).

- 'Finally, brothers, whatever is true, whatever is honourable, whatever is just, whatever is pure, whatever is lovely, whatever is commendable, if there is any excellence, if there is anything worthy of praise, think about these things' (Philippians 4:8 ESV).

- 'But as you excel in everything—in faith, in speech, in knowledge, in all earnestness, and in our love for you—see that you excel in this act of grace also' (2 Corinthians 8:7 ESV).

Faithfulness

- 'Let love and faithfulness never leave you; bind them round your neck, write them on the tablet of your heart' (Proverbs 3:3).

- 'See, the enemy is puffed up; his desires are not upright—but the righteous person will live by his faithfulness' (Habakkuk 2:4).

- 'For Jesus was faithful to God who appointed Him High Priest, just as Moses also faithfully served in God's house' (Hebrews 3:2 TLB).

- 'His master replied, "Well done, good and faithful servant! You have been faithful with a few things; I will put you in charge of many things. Come and share your master's happiness!"' (Matthew 25:21).

Forgiveness

- '"For if you forgive men when they sin against you, your heavenly Father will also forgive you, but if you do not forgive men their sins, your Father will not forgive your sins" (Matthew 6:14-15).

- "Then Peter came to Jesus and asked, "Lord, how many times shall I forgive my brother or sister who sins against me? Up to seven times?" Jesus answered, "I tell you, not seven times, but seventy times seven" (Matthew 18:21-22).

- "As far as the east is from the west, so far has He removed our transgressions from us" (Psalm 103:12).

- 'Bear with each other and forgive one another if any of you has a grievance against someone. Forgive as the Lord forgave you' (Colossians 3:13).

Generosity

- ✤ "If anyone forces you to go one mile, go with them two miles. Give to the one who asks you, and do not turn away from the one who wants to borrow from you" (Matthew 5:41-42).

- ✤ "Sell your possessions and give to the poor. Provide purses for yourselves that will not wear out, a treasure in heaven that will never fail, where no thief comes near and no moth destroys" (Luke 12:33).

- ✤ 'But Zacchaeus stood up and said to the Lord, "Look, Lord! Here and now I give half of my possessions to the poor, and if I have cheated anybody out of anything, I will pay back four times the amount" (Luke 19:8).

- ✤ "Remember this: Whoever sows sparingly will also reap sparingly, and whoever sows generously will also reap generously" (2 Corinthians 9:6).

Holiness

- ✤ "But just as He who called you is holy, so be holy in all you do; for it is written: 'Be holy, because I am holy" (1 Peter 1:15-16).

- ✤ "He has saved us and called us to a holy life, not because of anything we have done but because of His own purpose and grace. This grace was given us in Christ Jesus before the beginning of time" (2 Timothy 1:9).

- ✤ "Therefore, I urge you, brothers and sisters, in view of God's mercy, to offer your bodies as a living sacrifice, holy and pleasing to God, this is your true and proper worship" (Romans 12:1).

- ✤ "Make every effort to live in peace with everyone and to be holy; without holiness no one will see the Lord" (Hebrews 12:14).

Hospitality

- ✤ "They must enjoy having guests in their homes and must love all that is good. They must be sensible men, and fair. They must be clean minded and level headed" (Titus 1:8 TLB).

- ✤ "Offer hospitality to one another without grumbling" (1 Peter 4:9).

- ✤ "Do not forget to show hospitality to strangers, for by so doing some people have shown hospitality to angels without knowing it" (Hebrews 13:2).

- ✤ "Share with the Lord's people who are in need. Practise hospitality" (Romans 12:13).

Honouring Others

- ✤ "Be devoted to one another in love. Honour one another above yourselves" (Romans 12:10).

- ✤ "Honour your father and your mother, as the Lord your God has commanded you, so that you may live long and that it may go well with you in the land the Lord your God is giving you" (Deuteronomy 5:16).

- ✤ "Show respect for everyone. Love Christians everywhere. Fear God and honour the government" (1 Peter 2:17 TLB).

- ✤ "We are careful to be honourable before the Lord, but we also want everyone else to see that we are honourable" (2 Corinthians 8:21 NLT).

Honesty

- "Honesty guides good people; dishonesty destroys treacherous people" (Proverbs 11:3 NLT).
- "Simply let your 'Yes' be 'Yes' and your 'No' be 'No'; anything beyond this comes from the evil one" (Matthew 5:37 NIV 1984).
- "Righteous lips are the delight of a king, and he loves him who speaks what is right" (Proverbs 16:13 ESV).
- "The Lord detests the use of dishonest scales, but he delights in accurate weights" (Proverbs 11:1 NLT).

Humility

- "Be completely humble and gentle; be patient, bearing with one another in love" (Ephesians 4:2).
- "All of you, clothe yourselves with humility towards one another, because, "God opposes the proud but shows favour to the humble" (1 Peter 5:5b)
- "He guides the humble in what is right and teaches them His way" (Psalms 25:9).
- "For all those who exalt themselves will be humbled, and those who humble themselves will be exalted" (Luke 14:11)

Justice

- "But let justice roll on like a river, righteousness like a never-failing stream!" (Amos 5:24).
- "He has shown you, O mortal, what is good. And what does the Lord require of you? To act justly and to love mercy and to walk humbly with your God" (Micah 6:8).
- "For I, the Lord, love justice; I hate robbery and wrongdoing" (Isaiah 61:8a).
- "Learn to do right; seek justice. Defend the oppressed. Take up the cause of the fatherless; plead the case of the widow." (Isaiah 1:17)

Kindness

- "Whoever is kind to the poor lends to the Lord, and He will reward them for what they have done" (Proverbs 19:17).
- "Love is patient, love is kind. It does not envy, it does not boast, it is not proud" (1 Corinthians 13:4).
- "Therefore, as God's chosen people, holy and dearly loved, clothe yourselves with compassion, kindness, humility, gentleness and patience" (Colossians 3:12).
- "Be kind and compassionate to one another, forgiving each other, just as in Christ God forgave you" (Ephesians 4:32).

Obedience

- "He replied, "Blessed rather are those who hear the word of God and obey it" (Luke 11:28).
- "And this is love: that we walk in obedience to His commands. As you have heard from the beginning, His command is that you walk in love" (2 John 1:6).
- "And being found in appearance as a man, he humbled himself by becoming obedient to death, even death on a cross!" (Philippians 2:8).
- "Father, if You are willing, take this cup from me; yet not my will, but Yours be done" (Luke 22:42).

Patience

- "A hot-tempered person stirs up conflict, but the one who is patient calms a quarrel" (Proverbs 15:18).
- "The end of a matter is better than its beginning, and patience is better than pride" (Ecclesiastes 7:8).
- "Let us not become weary in doing good, for at the proper time we will reap a harvest if we do not give up" (Galatians 6:9).
- "Be still before the Lord and wait patiently for Him" (Psalm 37:7a)

Peace

- "Do not be anxious about anything, but in every situation, by prayer and petition, with thanksgiving, present your requests to God. And the peace of God, which transcends all understanding, will guard your hearts and your minds in Christ Jesus" (Philippians 4:6-7).
- "Let the peace of Christ rule in your hearts, since as members of one body you were called to peace. And be thankful" (Colossians 3:15).
- "The mind governed by the flesh is death, but the mind governed by the Spirit is life and peace" (Romans 8:6).
- "Blessed are the peacemakers, for they will be called children of God" (Matthew 5:9).

Servanthood

- "For who is greater, the one who is at the table or the one who serves? Is it not the one who is at the table? But I am among you as one who serves" (Luke 22:27).
- "Whoever serves me must follow me; and where I am, my servant also will be. My Father will honour the one who serves me" (John 12:26).
- "Live as free people, but do not use your freedom as a cover-up for evil; live as God's slaves" (1 Peter 2:16).
- "For even the Son of Man came not to be served but to serve, and to give His life as a ransom for many" (Mark 10:45).

Stewardship

- "Each of you should use whatever gift you have received to serve others, as faithful stewards of God's grace in its various forms" (1 Peter 4:10).
- "Whatever you do, work at it with all your heart, as working for the Lord, not for human masters" (Colossians 3:23).
- "If you are faithful in little things, you will be faithful in large ones. But if you are dishonest in little things, you won't be honest with greater responsibilities" (Luke 16:10 NLT).
- "But seek first His kingdom and His righteousness, and all these things will be given to you as well" (Matthew 6:33).

Trustworthiness

- 'The Lord detests lying lips, but He delights in people who are trustworthy" (Proverbs 12:22).

- "Love does not delight in evil but rejoices with the truth" (1 Corinthians 13:6).

- "But blessed is the one who trusts in the Lord, whose confidence is in Him" (Jeremiah 17:7).

- "These are the things you are to do: Speak the truth to each other, and render true and sound judgment in your courts; do not plot evil against each other, and do not love to swear falsely. I hate all this," declares the Lord" (Zechariah 8:16-17).

Unity

- "Again, truly I tell you that if two of you on earth agree about anything they ask for, it will be done for them by my Father in heaven. For where two or three gather in my name, there am I with them" (Matthew 18:19-20).

- "Make every effort to keep the unity of the Spirit through the bond of peace" (Ephesians 4:3).

- "I in them and You in me—so that they may be brought to complete unity. Then the world will know that You sent me and have loved them even as You have loved me" (John 17:23).

- "How good and pleasant it is when God's people live together in unity!" (Psalm 133:1).

ENDNOTES

Copyright

1. (p.iv) Unless indicated otherwise, Scripture quotations are taken from the Holy Bible, New International Version® Anglicised, NIV® Copyright © 1979, 1984, 2011 by Biblica, Inc.® Used by permission. All rights reserved worldwide.

Scripture quotations marked ESV are from the Holy Bible, English Standard Version. ESV® Text Edition: 2016. Copyright © 2001 by Crossway Bibles, a publishing ministry of Good News Publishers. Used by permission. All rights reserved worldwide.

Scripture quotations marked NLT are from the Holy Bible, New Living Translation, copyright © 1996, 2004, 2015 by Tyndale House Foundation. Used by permission of Tyndale House Publishers, Inc., Carol Stream, Illinois 60188. All rights reserved.

Scripture quotations marked MSG are from The Message Copyright © 1993, 2002, 2018 by Eugene H. Peterson. Used by permission of NavPress, represented by Tyndale House Publishers. All rights reserved.

Scripture quotations marked TLB are from The Living Bible copyright © 1971 by Tyndale House Foundation. Used by permission of Tyndale House Publishers Inc., Carol Stream, Illinois 60188. All rights reserved.

Introduction

1. (p.4) Ken Costa, God at Work: Living Every Day with Purpose (Alpha International, 2013)

Module One - Gifts

1. (p.13) 16personalities.com (NERIS Analytics Limited) www.16personalities.com/free-personality-test accessed 24/22/21

Module Three - Abilities

1. (p.50) Max Lucado, Cure for the Common Life (Max Lucado; Reprint edition 2011)

2. (p.60) Cappfinity's Strengths Profile Assessment, www.strengthsprofile.com

Module Four - Curiosities

1. (p.80) [p76] Howard Gardener, Howard Gardener's Official Authoritative Site of Multiple Intelligences, (MI Oasis) https://www.multipleintelligencesoasis.org/a-beginners-guide-to-mi (accessed 22/06/2021)

2. (p.84) [80] Holland Code, Wikipedia, (Wikimedia Foundation, Inc) https://en.wikipedia.org/wiki/Holland_Codes (accessed 31/05/22)

Module Five - Experiences

1. (p.103) [100] Lexico.com (Oxford University Press) https://www.lexico.com/definition/achievement accessed 29/06/2021

2. (p.110) The University of Edinburgh (The University of Edinburgh) https://www.ed.ac.uk/reflection/reflectors-toolkit/reflecting-on-experience/carl pub 09/11/2018 (accessed 29/06/2021)

Appendix One

1. (p.156) Your SHAPE for God's Service, Amiel Mary E.Osmaston, (Arthur Rank Centre), https://arthurrankcentre.org.uk/resources/your-shape-for-gods-service/your-shape-for-gods-service-full-course-2013-version/ accessed 31/05/2021 3rd Edition

2. (p.156) Erik Rees, S.H.A.P.E: Finding and Fulfilling Your Unique Purpose in Life, (Zondervan) 2006

ACKNOWLEDGEMENTS

I didn't anticipate publishing another book quite so soon after my first book God's GRACE for Your Career, but as I chatted with people who had read it, I realised there was nowhere to scribble in it, nowhere to answer the many questions I posed in the activities. And so, the idea for the learning guide was born. I wanted somewhere people could keep all their thoughts, ideas, reflections in one place .

My particular thanks go to Abbirose Adey who came up with the styling for this learning guide with her invaluable suggestions for the use of colour, spacing and icons. She guided me through the editing and proofing with a keen eye for detail alongside an understanding of the requirements for a learning guide. I am amazed by her ingenuity and resilience and am grateful for her support and her never ending encouragement.

My thanks also go to my husband Mark whose illustrations are used again in this learning guide and who painstakingly proofread it and asked if there was enough space to write the answers. His patience and support are a mainstay in my life.

Thanks also to Pete Gray who didn't bat an eyelid when I said I needed an adaptation of the wonderful cover he designed for God's GRACE for Your Career. I'm delighted with the result.

I also want to thank my trusted friends, you know who you are, who prayerfully encouraged me to produce this learning guide, endorsing what my readers were saying. I am forever indebted by their prayers and support.

None of this would have been possible without our Heavenly Father and the inner wisdom He gave me to write God's GRACE for Your Career and the prompting to produce this learning guide. It really is true, 'delight yourself in the Lord and He will give you the desires of your heart' (Psalm 37:4).

ABOUT KATIE CONLEY

Engaging, dedicated, insightful - this is how Katie's clients describe her and the career coaching she offers. Katie is a licensed Career Coach, accredited Strengths Profile© practitioner, a registered professional with the Career Development Institute and an associate member of the Chartered Institute of Personnel and Development.

Throughout her varied career the times she's enjoyed the most are when she has been talking with people about what they do and why! Katie has managed graduate recruitment programmes, delivered career development workshops, created personal development plans, provided career coaching and delivered lots of skills development training. She's been a sales assistant, waitress, training officer, head of department, non-exec director and director of her own learning and development consulting business, all of which has brought her into contact with a wide range of people. She has always been keen to learn about the choices people make for their working lives and help them make changes, learn new things, or take on new challenges.

She set up Conley Career Coaching to specifically continue her passion for helping people progress in their careers, whether this is helping them make choices for their next career move or helping someone back into work following a career break, discussing career options, putting together a job search strategy, advising on CVs or doing some interview practice.

Katie has been a Christian for over 20 years. She has a certificate in Christian Discipleship and oversees home groups for her church, as well as running two of them. She has led several Alpha courses (for those exploring the Christian faith) and is also on the prayer ministry team. Katie is very comfortable discussing career choices from a Christian viewpoint and loves to see how our faith interacts with our career choices and what God has planned for us.

She would love to hear your experiences too!

Contact Katie directly via these links:

www.conleycareercoaching.com/

linkedin.com/in/katieconley-careercoach/

facebook.com/conleycareercoaching

twitter.com/ConleyCareers

www.instagram.com/katieconleycareercoach/

CAREER COACHING OPTIONS

Be clear about your career direction.

The path to career clarity is different for everyone and tailored to your specific needs. This series of 1-to-1 personalised coaching always involves a voyage of self-discovery to help you unpack your career toolkit so you can be clear about what you've got followed by visioning your future career, assessing your resources and making a career plan.

Clients gain increased confidence in their future career options.

Career Change

Don't leave your career change to chance!

If you're serious about making a career change and determined to invest the time and effort required, then over a few months you will undertake a thorough and detailed exploration of what you want and discover how to take steps to achieve your vision for your future career.

Clients will be equipped with practical ideas and know the steps to take to realise their career dreams.

Job Search

Gain confidence in your job search.

Not everyone enjoys job searching, and many people don't know where to start. Designed around you, job search coaching includes support and advice on the job search process including job search strategy, creating an up-to-date relevant CV/LinkedIn profile, networking, the application process and preparing for interviews.

Clients will be able to search for a new job with confidence and courage.

Christian Career Coaching

Explore career options from a faith perspective.

Explore and discuss your career choices and challenges from a Christian perspective with space to pray and discern God's purpose and plans for your career. Many Christians find it really helpful to be able to discuss their career from a Christian perspective without feeling they have to censor their words or thoughts.

Contact Katie for a free 1-1 consultation to see how she can help you.

Conley Career Coaching

TURN OVER A NEW LEAF

NOTES UNWRAPPED

Use these pages for additional notes, thoughts or prayers which come to your throughout your learning journey.

Milton Keynes UK
Ingram Content Group UK Ltd.
UKHW051119301123
433543UK00001B/2